To Tina —

Freedom!

Hamody Jasim
Iraqi Soldier American Spy

The

Terrorist

Whisperer

The Story of the Pro American

A True Story by

Hamody Jasim

Dedication

This book is dedicated to all the men and women who fought tirelessly side by side against terrorism and to preserve freedom. Your sacrifices will never be forgotten. Until we meet again...

In Memoriam of my good friend who was the first female USMC officer killed in combat during the Iraq war:

Major Megan McClung

The Terrorist Whisperer

Library of Congress

ISBN-13   978-1508923671

ISBN-10   1508923671

Contents

Author's Note

The events in this book are true events, and my personal experiences which occurred over many years. Some of the people's identities have been protected due to the sensitivity of their jobs and current military active duty. I have not used any classified information in this book. A copy of this book has been sent to the Department of Defense for security review and it has been cleared.

"Sergeant Major Hamody Jasim and many of his peers in Iraq's noncommissioned officer corps developed very close professional relationships with the U.S. and coalition officers who worked with the Iraqi Security Forces. This was particularly evident during the Surge and the following two years. These young Iraqi leaders served their country and all Iraqis very impressively, proving instrumental in the development of the Iraqi capabilities as Iraqi and coalition units fought to reduce the levels of violence that escalated so terribly in 2006 and into 2007. The subsequent reduction in the violence was a tribute not just to the U.S. and coalition units, but to their Iraqi counterparts, as well. It was tragic in 2012 and 2013 to see many of Iraq's commissioned and noncommissioned officers leave the Iraqi forces and, in many cases, Iraq as well, when government actions led to a return of sectarian mistrust and violence, and did such damage to the fabric of the Iraqi society and its Army and Police units."

RET. General David H. Petraeus U.S. Army

1

Growing up in Iraq

The saying, "A day's work is never done" could not be truer growing up and living in Iraq. You had to work hard to survive. But looking back at all the good times and the bad, I am not sure I would change one minute of it. All of it shaped me and made me who I am today. I have learned to appreciate life and I am grateful for what God has given me. As I reflect on my family, my friends, everyone who I lost in combat, the terrorists I fought and everything I endured, these unique experiences made me into someone who would fight evil on any soil.

I have been called a "terrorist whisperer." According to the dictionary to call one's self a "whisperer" you need to be able to excel at calming or training hard-to-manage people or animals using non-coercive methods based on an understanding of the animal's or person's natural instincts.

I was called a "terrorist whisperer" by people I worked with and helped when their family member or child had been kidnapped. In my heart I wanted to help because I didn't want to see another person die for no reason at the hands of the terrorists. But, after my story, I will let you decide. A terrorist is someone who operates behind a curtain to scare others and gain power through fear and intimidation. I would go behind the curtain, understand what their motive was, find out their identity, family tribe, and their greatest weakness. Many of these terrorists are promised rewards if they carry out evil actions. I find nothing rewarding in taking someone's life. Life is wonderful, precious and meaningful. To me if you take an innocent life you are nothing more than a coward.

In Iraq death was an everyday occurrence while growing up under Saddam's reign and administration. People's lives were taken like they meant nothing. I would look at the people who had died and I thought about all the people they left behind. Their parents, spouse, children, friends and extended family. A huge void which would never be filled. I hated seeing people die. These people were good people and had every reason in the world to live. As a kid I saw more death then I should have. No child should ever see the amount of death and destruction I saw. Growing up under Saddam Hussein was a tough time. He controlled the country by using terrorism. You lived scared and you felt like you couldn't even trust the walls in your house around you.

His people were all over the place and they would kill for no reason. We lived in such a controlled society. When I grew up I knew I didn't want to live like this. There was something inside of me that wanted much more than this. I hated these people who would terrorize my family. I wanted to get rid of them and I did my best to make my wish a reality.

My Family

My life story doesn't feel like much of one sometimes. I came from a loving home who always supported me one hundred percent on whatever I wanted to do. I did challenge my parents at times though. I was born in Baghdad, Iraq, and lucky enough to be a New Year's baby. I speak fluent Arabic and all the different dialects, Farsi and English. I have a Sunni mother and a Shiite father. I have 3 older siblings: my sisters Rana and Hala, and my brother Ayad. Growing up my parents were not very religious at all. We were always taught to do what was right, always help others, and God will show you the way. Be fair, kind and always be able to explain your actions. My siblings all went on to college and got degrees. My oldest sister became a world class musician. My brother works in IT and now resides in the U.S. And, my other sister became a biologist. They all have children now and they carry out the same beliefs my parents taught us.

My father, Jasim, is a very educated man. He served in the Infantry in the Iraqi military back in the 1970s. He went to college in England and he studied the English language further. He also traveled the world going to many different countries where he studied the people and their different cultures. My father's father, my grandfather, spoke English as well. He learned English from the British when they were in Iraq back in 1921. The British were in Iraq following the 1920 Iraqi Revolt against the proposed British mandate of Mesopotamia. When he was a kid he would try to talk to the soldiers in town. He was only able to use his hands, make signals and show them what he meant. The soldiers started to give him a couple of words a day to learn. After months of them being there my grandfather was able to make broken sentences, but he was able to speak some English. So as a gift the British gave him books to learn how to speak English to further his English language education and fluency. He was so excited to learn this new language. He started to teach his brothers how to speak English too. He showed them the books he had and once they got to a certain point, one brother, my dad's uncle, decided to go to the University of Baghdad and further his English language education. This uncle was the one who enhanced my dad's English language skills. My dad ended up going to the same university as his uncle. My grandfather made sure all his children learned English. He felt it was important for them to succeed. All of my grandfather's children, all nine of them went on and obtained college degrees and made something of themselves. The experience of learning English made them want to further their education because they enjoyed studying and learning. This is how my siblings and I learned the English language and why I learned to speak it so well. But during Saddam times you could not use or speak the English language. You could only speak Arabic. If you spoke English on the street you would get arrested. Saddam considered English the language of the enemy.

In 1980, a year after Saddam came to power, the Iran-Iraq war started. My father was a military intelligence officer in the Iraqi Army prior to Saddam coming to power. When Saddam came to power he changed a lot of positions of people in the military. Saddam brought people in to the military who had no military back ground at all, and put them into positions for which they had no discernable experience. These were members of his Ba'ath party and his own family members. My father worked for Saddam's brother-in-law, Adnan, while he was an officer. My father continued to work in the Iraqi military as an officer until 1992. Adnan was a great guy. He was a real people person. Saddam saw how the Iraqi people loved Adnan and it worried him because Adnan could become a future president at some point and take his power. So, Saddam executed Adnan, and Adnan's wife never spoke to him again after.

At the end of the Gulf War Saddam started conducting background checks on each military member. He did this after many Iraqis fought against the government when the Americans were in Iraq. If Saddam found out one or more of your family members was anti-government, or had been executed due to being anti-government, you were released from the Military. My dad was placed under investigation and put in jail for six months leaving my mom to take care of all of us. It had been discovered one of his brothers was anti-government and had been executed. After the investigation he was fired from the Military and sent home. I do not remember why my uncle was executed. I was only a baby and my dad never spoke too much about it. Had they found any evidence my dad had communication with any of the family members who were anti-government my dad would have been executed. In 1993, my dad received a mandatory order to re-enlist in the Iraqi Army. He was ordered to work an academic job where he was to teach cadets about foreign languages.

This new job my dad had been appointed to by Saddam did not pay enough to support our family. As punishment for having family members who were anti-government Saddam would make you work hard for little money. My father would work his day job, come home eat a quick dinner and leave to work as a taxi driver all night long. After driving for hours he came home, slept for a couple hours and went back to his job in the military. He worked

18

this schedule, six days a week for ten years, until 2003. He wanted to make sure my siblings' college was paid for. Education was a top priority for my father. My parents sold everything they had of value. Gold, appliances and anything else they could find for us to survive. For years we ate and survived off of potatoes, tomato soup and rice. It was hard times. Every month the government would give you rice, oil, flour and milk. Each person in the family was entitled to their portion of it and to this day they still receive it. Meat was expensive. We only ate meat once or twice a week. Saddam pretty much crushed us. But as a family, we stuck together and we got through.

My mom, unlike my dad, doesn't speak a word of English. She is a housewife with Turkish and Arab back grounds and she speaks both Turkish and Arabic. She dedicated her whole life to taking care of my dad and our family and she is still carrying on those responsibilities to this day. She likes to travel to the South of Iraq to get out of the city and away from all the current turmoil there now. The South of Iraq is quiet, peaceful and beautiful. My mom is one of the bravest women I know. She stayed by my dad's side through everything. They are married almost 40 years and they have been through it all! I think my mom goes to the South of Iraq to take a break from my dad now since he is no longer working and making her crazy, but she would never admit it. Today in Baghdad you take your life in your hands walking to the market to buy tomatoes or attend social events.

This is due to suicide bombers and car bombs. No one knows when or where a bomb is going to go off. For safer personal communication today social media has become a way of life in Iraq instead of meeting up at a coffee shop to chat. You can still socialize and chat with others, and you don't have to leave your home or risk your life doing so.

Al-Hay

I went to school in Baghdad. During breaks from school I would always go to the south of Iraq. My grandfather's farm was located in Al-Hay, Iraq. I loved it there. It was a quiet simple life. People took care of their farms and animals, and education was very important. I loved it over the city life. Your neighbors were like family. Everyone helped each other out. I would help tend to my grandfather's animals and play with them. He had cows, sheep, camels, chickens, turkeys, goats and so many others. For an Arab man it is an honorable duty to protect your animals from other wild animals, such as wolves. The wolf, in my opinion, is one of the smartest animals I had ever seen. They were so coordinated when they would close in on their prey. My grandfather used an electric fence to keep the sheep together. Those wolves would know where the electric fence was and how to go around it. The wolf would sneak in and grab the sheep at its throat so it couldn't yell. It would guide the sheep where to go as he held it in his mouth. It was like the wolf studied mine and the sheep's movements, and it knew when to strike. He would see me out there watching over the herd. As my eyes would start to get heavy in the early morning hours from being up all night the wolf would strike. I loved watching the wolf's behavior and actions. I would feel bad if I had to shoot at the wolf because the wolf taught me a lot of lessons. The greatest lesson he taught me was when it was the right time to strike. I learned to strike the moment people turned their head or lowered their guard. Strike when it was not expected. What I found fascinating was if a wolf got injured and was bleeding he would be eliminated from the pack. You never saw an injured wolf come back.

I was so fascinated with the wolf. I was so interested in how it operated and its mannerisms. It made me study all the other animals too and understand their behaviors. This is how I learned how to protect the animals at a young age. It was a huge responsibility for me, but I was honored to do it for my grandfather. It was at this time I learned how to shoot a gun, and my first gun was an AK-47. My grandfather gave it to me and the gun was bigger than I was, but I could protect those animals like nobody's business.

The upbringing I had in the country taught me how to use my senses which enabled me to learn how to read and listen to animals. I learned if you ran away from the dangerous animal, they would run after you. But if you ran towards the animal, they didn't know what to do and they would run away. Little did I know my education in animal mannerisms would serve me later on in life when I would use it studying people. The one thing I noticed was humans and animals had similar natural instincts and mannerisms. I found my education on the animals helpful later on in life.

Fighting for Survival

I had a childhood, which was good when I was in the south of Iraq, but it was a constant fight for survival in the city of Baghdad. It was survival because of war, Saddam Hussein and the Ba'ath party. We had the same regime and shit in the south, but it was not as constant. The south of Iraq was a large Shiite area. There were some Sunni's and both the Sunni's and some Shiites were part of the Ba'ath party. Saddam relied on them to keep control in the south. There were some political issues in the south, but not as many like in the city of Baghdad where Saddam spent most of his time.

In the city we had many more eyes on us from Saddam's Regime, Ba'ath party members and Police. There was a lot of pressure on people who were not allies with any of Saddam's political parties. My dad had built our home in a nice area of Baghdad. It was a more upscale neighborhood. It was a beautiful spot. But there was only one problem with it. Because it was a nicer neighborhood there were a lot of Ba'ath party members there. Most of our neighbors around us were Ba'ath party members. So we were always watched. I was harassed and picked on at school by their kids. These kids were exact mirrors of their parents. They would watch their parents bully and beat the shit out of other people. So, these kids learned it was okay to do this. Military guards would drive these kids to school and open the car doors for them. The teachers would be scared of these kids. Some kids at ages twelve to fourteen would bring guns to school and keep them in a holster. Nobody could ever say anything to them because they felt they were above the law and were untouchable. There was this one Ba'athist kid at school and he picked on me every day. One day after school he and his friends knocked me to the ground and kept kicking me in head. When they stopped I had ringing in my ears and a head ache every day for two months. I took this shit every day and I sucked it up. I didn't want my parents to get in trouble or be hurt by their parents. One day he was giving me shit and slapping me in the back of the head. It was at this moment I lost it and beat the shit out of him. I had found a piece of wood with two nails in it behind the school, and I wacked him hard with it in his back. He screamed and fell to the ground. I did get in trouble, but my dad knew how it was for me. I was kicked out of school and had to go to another one. But this boy never gave me shit again. The Ba'ath party members were the ugliest and greediest people I knew. They had the best of everything and treated everyone else like garbage. During our hard times they would give my poor mom a hard time about feeding us vegetables and no meat. They were cold people. They were the pure product of Saddam's ugliness.

2

Gulf War, 1991

My greatest memories of war and survival start back in 1991. This is my earliest memory I can remember of surviving Saddam's Regime. I had lost many family members, cousins and uncles to the Regime because they were against or thought to be against the government. I remember my grandfather speaking of the loss of his two youngest sons who were in pharmacy school. The two young men had done nothing wrong or against the government. They were so busy with school they didn't have time to do anything else. They were executed because they were professionals and it was assumed they were against the government because of our family history. There used to be a saying that the Ba'ath party would execute you with their pens. If a Ba'ath party member didn't like you, they would write up these false reports, hand it off a higher level member and the punishment would be handed down. The report could be fabricated but if it came from a higher level member you couldn't do anything about it.

The assumption by Saddam was if you felt this way about the government it was a guarantee the rest of your family felt the same way too. The Regime would go to relatives' homes to question them about the family member who was against the government. They would look for any pictures of the anti-government relative in your house, and any recent correspondence with them. If the Regime found any pictures or correspondence which was recent with the family member you were executed also. It was the worst way to live. A family member had been taken from you and you had to pretend you didn't know the person, which made the loss of the relative even worse. You felt like you were deceiving the family in some way.

It was March or April 1991 and nearing the end of the Gulf War. My dad was in Kuwait with the mandatory Iraqi Military. He didn't have any choice because if he didn't serve he would be killed. This war started because Saddam had decided to occupy Kuwait. Saddam had told the military, before the war started, they were going to do military drills and exercises at the border of Kuwait and Iraq with live ammunition. No sooner they got there Saddam made an order to invade Kuwait. Hence, the Gulf War started.

Soon after the Iraqi Military invaded Kuwait, the U.S. Military came in to defend Kuwait and defeat Saddam. The U.S. was successful in accomplishing this and forcing the Iraqi Military out by using air strikes. As the U.S. Military worked their way through the South of Iraq, on their way north towards Baghdad, the Shiite rebels followed behind and started attacking Ba'ath party members to continue the liberation of Iraq. All of a sudden the U.S. Military started to withdraw back to Kuwait. This surprised the rebels and the Iraqi people because they thought the U.S. was going to go all the way to Baghdad. The withdrawal of the U.S. left the people in the south of Iraq vulnerable.

My mom, three siblings and I went to the South of Iraq to live at my Grandfather's farm near the end of the Gulf war. We needed to take a break from all the chaos and bombings in Baghdad. The bombing going on in Baghdad was due to the U. S. Military going after Saddam's Republican Guard and his allies. As we got to the South of Iraq, the Iraqi people and Shiite rebels began a revolution against Saddam's Republican Guard and Ba'ath party to help liberate Iraq.

Mass Killings

It was at this time Saddam and his leaders started to seek revenge against the people in the South of Iraq. They were being punished for working with the U.S. Military and going against him. Saddam called them traitors and put Ali Hassan al-Majid (Chemical Ali) and his son, Qusay Hussein

27

in charge of taking out all the Iraqi people in the South of Iraq. They accomplished this by using the Republican Guard who were stationed in Baghdad at the time.

Chemical Ali was Saddam's cousin and one of his generals in the military. Saddam would use Chemical Ali when he needed large numbers of people to be killed. He was known for the al-Anfal Campaign in the final stages of the Iraq-Iran war. The al-Anfal Campaign was known as one of the greatest crimes against humanity. Surat al-Anfal in the Qur'an was a name used by the former Iraqi Ba'athist government for a series of systematic attacks against the Kurdish population in northern Iraq between1986-1989. He killed thousands of people using chemicals. The exact number of people killed we did not know. It has been stated it was around one hundred thousand men, women and children. However, there was death and destruction brought to four thousand five hundred villages and complete massacre of the people in those villages. At the time Chemical Ali would have used chemicals on us to kill all of us, like he did to the Kurds, but the United Nations Security Council warned them to not use any chemicals. The Iraqi Military also had a no-fly zone imposed on them by the U.S. Military. This pissed Chemical Ali off even more and instead Saddam's Republican Guard was used to invade. Saddam felt the people in the entire South of Iraq were traitors and they must die. This would soon lead to the Mass Killing Campaign.

There was a one star general at the time named General Mohan. He was a mean bastard and he was happy to carry out killing the rebels and people in the south of Iraq. Remember his name because I can assure you his name will come up again and again. General Mohan was an intelligence officer for Saddam in 1986. Saddam sent Mohan to train in Russia for four years. He came back in 1990 to Saddam's military and he was one of the secret intelligence commanders.

There was no television or cable in Iraq. We only had a radio. At first the Americans on the ground were telling people to please leave and evacuate. They knew the Republican Guard was going to start moving forward and people would be killed. No sooner the Americans were telling people to leave, Chemical Ali came on over the radio and started making threats. The elders in the area didn't listen to the Americans. They felt they had done nothing wrong and they weren't going to leave their land.

When people realized the Americans pulled out, they became afraid, and used this opportunity to run to the borders of Kuwait and Saudi Arabia to seek refuge with the American Military. This is why so many Iraqis came to the U.S. in 1991. My grandfather said this was our land, we did nothing wrong and we were going to fight. There was also a common feeling among the people that this was a way for Saddam to make people leave their homes, in which he would come in and take their property. But, my mom also didn't want to leave because we didn't know where my dad was and she didn't want to leave him behind. So as the Republican Guard entered they used tanks, and infantry on the ground with large empty trucks behind them. They would use these empty trucks to take people from the villages and dump them in large mass graves dug and waiting. They separated the men from the women and children. The men were lined up and shot. The women, children and elders were taken to the mass graves. These people they were killing had done nothing wrong. They were not rebels. They hadn't fought against the government. They were simple people living in the villages.

To The Swamp

As we watched the Republican Guard get closer to my grandfather's house. Everyone started getting nervous. They were about one mile away. My uncles and family felt hopeless. My mom had such a look of fear on her face. I will never forget it. She looked at my siblings and I and kissed us all on the forehead. She told us how much she loved us. We all felt like this was it. My grandfather all of a sudden yelled "Run to the swamp!" The swamp was located at the edge of my grandfather's fields. It was about a quarter of a mile away from the house. It wasn't close but it wasn't real far either. My mother, uncles, cousins and all the family ran. I never ran so fast in my life. There were other people from the village running through my grandfather's land to get to the swamps also. The Republican guard had started to launch mortars at us. The mortars were hitting all over the place. They wanted no one to live. My grandfather told us to run zig-zag. This way if the Guard launched mortars at us they would miss us and we would make it to the water. As we were running, there were other children running next to me from the village. These were the neighbor's children running for their lives to the swamp to seek refuge also. A mortar had landed killing two of the children running next to me and injuring another. One child stopped to pick them up and keep them with us, but they were dead. There was one young boy who was injured, but he kept running. We arrived at the swamp. As we were getting into the boats, this young boy was in bad shape and we had to help him into the boat. He had a hole in the right side of his body from the shrapnel. I remember seeing lots of blood. The women in the boat tried to save him but he didn't make it. As my uncles started rowing us deeper into the swamps a helicopter appeared over our head. All of us were scared. We looked at each other as if to say this was it, this was our time. Instead, the pilot started shooting in the other direction as he looked at us. It became obvious to us the pilot didn't want to kill anyone. Instead, he pretended he was shooting at us and flew away. This gave us a chance to get away and get under the plants in the water. Another helicopter came over us, and this pilot wanted us dead. But, he didn't see us under the plants. He did destroy our boats and did shoot anything he could. People were jumping out of the boats and swimming as fast as they could. He was successful in killing some people. These are images I will never forget. I was so scared. I didn't understand why this was happening. We lived in the swamp for four nights. Our only means of survival was to fish and make cover out of the reeds in the water.

Over the next couple of days you could still hear the gun shots, the military vehicles moving and people yelling. All of a sudden it became silent. It was on the fourth night that two of my uncles decided to swim under the cover of the night back to my grandfather's house. They wanted to know if any of the Republican Guard were still there. When they got there the whole village was dark. There was no sign of life. The only sign of life was the wolves eating the dead bodies. These were the bodies of our friends and our neighbors. I knew them as my south of Iraq family. My uncles dug shallow graves to temporarily bury the dead so they would not get eaten and have a proper burial. These were people my family knew for years and my uncles wanted to treat their bodies with the most respect. Many people I knew and grew up with were murdered. Some were able to escape like us but there was a huge loss of life. As I explained before, your neighbors were like family. For me it was so hard to understand as a kid what had happened. People were murdered in Karbala, Nasiriya and 12 other states out of 18 states. As a family we took it day by day. We went back to my grandfather's farm and started to put what we could back together. The

Republican Guard had taken his animals, which they used for food. They had ransacked his whole house. They had destroyed it. So each day we worked from morning to night. Over a month had gone by. The Republican Guard had not come back. It was at this time my mom wanted to head back to Baghdad. We had to wait for some type of normal life and transportation to be restored. Life there was far from the normal we knew. Even after we returned back to Baghdad we were still looked at as traitors. It was a general concensus in the Saddam administration if you were from or had family in the south of Iraq, you were against the government. I am not sure of the exact numbers but I do know a few hundred thousand people lost their lives to the mass killings. Some families were buried all together. To this day mass graves are still being found with bodies in them. These graves were massive holes dug into the dessert. Some so big they even buried the trucks with the people in them. It is unknown how many mass graves there were and where their exact locations are. Families still search to this day hoping to find the remains of their loved ones. There could be many more graves still waiting to be found. Saddam did all this to teach the Iraqi people a lesson. From 1991 all the way through 2003 there were no more rebels or uprisings against the government. Saddam made an example out of these people to show others what would happen to them if they tried to rise up against the government.

3

12-Year-Old Political Prisoner

The Ba'ath party was very strong and Saddam was ruthless. After what happened in the south the government started checking out family records and investigating which family members had gone against the government. This is why my dad lost his military position and went to jail for six months as I explained before. There was segregation between the Shiites and the Ba'ath party. If you were a Shiite or a Kurd you were not trusted. In every neighborhood there was a Ba'ath party member. This person would report back anything to the intelligence committee which looked against the government. We were always under watch. If you got hit, you couldn't hit back. You couldn't defend yourself because it would come back to you in some way. My brother was often in trouble with them. He would argue with our next door neighbor who was a Ba'ath party member. He would snoop around our house all the time. My brother would get so frustrated with him and we were thankful my brother was never thrown in jail or harmed for how he yelled at this guy.

I was twelve years old when I learned the hardest lesson about the Ba'ath party.

The Ba'athist Police Officer

I was on my way home from school one afternoon. I was walking with a couple of good friends of mine. We were laughing and joking around, minding our own business. As we were walking past a couple of police officers on the street corner one of them stopped us. The officer asked me if I had any money on me. I told him I didn't. I did have some money on me but I didn't want him to know. I had 500 dinar on me. At the time it was equal to about five dollars in the U.S. Half of the money was in my wallet and the other half was hidden in my clothes. I did this because I knew this would happen at some point. He also asked me if I had any cigarettes. I told him I didn't smoke. The police felt they had power to rob people on the street and you couldn't defend yourself at all. This was a common thing the police did. He asked me a second time if I had any money. I told the officer again I didn't have any money on me. The next thing I knew he hit me hard and it hurt. So I cursed back at him about his sister and he pushed me to the ground. He started searching me and found the money. The officer got pissed and told me how he could make a case for me to get me executed. Little did I know this particular officer happened to be a higher rank in the Ba'ath party and his last name was al Dulaimi. Remember this family tribe name you may see it come up again and again. The officer cuffed us, put us in a truck and told us he would be taking us to jail. He took my two friends and I to a special security place for people who were anti-government. Can you imagine 3 twelve year olds who were anti-government? But this is the shit we had to deal with. He took us to The Internal State Security Secret Police under the Ministry of the Interior. On the way to this facility, the two other police officers with him said "He is a kid, let him go."

He responded back to these police officers, "No, I am going to put in a report and have him executed, and if you say anything more I will have you executed also."

This ugly officer forced the other two officers to sign a false report. When I got to the facility I found out the officer wrote down I had attacked him and hurt him. I weighed one hundred pounds wet. He was over six feet tall and built muscular wise. The whole thing was a bunch of bullshit. And you couldn't do a damn thing about it. You had no voice. You were guilty and nobody cared. I knew my parents would be worried when I didn't come home after school and I had no way to contact them.

As I walked down the hallway of the jail it was dark and I was scared. I was being hit by the stock of a gun multiple times. I was hit on the back of my head and my upper back. It seemed like it was coming at me from all directions but I couldn't see where it was coming from. Walking down the hallway lasted forever. After going through all this, they threw me into a cell. The cell was gigantic. It was like a warehouse with bars around it and a cement floor. There were no beds or toilet like when you think of a jail cell. My two friends were there with me also. I felt so bad they got tangled up in this mess because they were with me. They never said anything to the officer. It was so unfair for them to be there. None of us deserved to be there. Even thought we were all kids they treated us like adults. I looked at the school books I had been carrying with me through all this and thought to myself I will never be using those again. I missed my mom and dad so much. I was so worried I would never see them again. All kinds of thoughts run through your head when you are picked up as political prisoner knowing you might never see the light of day again and your body hurts so bad from being beaten.

Many of the inmates asked us why we were there. They couldn't understand why we were so young and placed in this type of jail. The jail we were in was a special jail for interrogations. This jail detained anti-government people and specialized in beatings and torture to get confessions from people. When I told them I wouldn't give the cop my money they all yelled at me. One inmate said, "You give him your fucking money! If they ask you for your pants, give them your fucking pants! Don't argue with them. They will fuck you up!

We are all here for political reasons, this is not a life you want. Don't fight them back. Give them what they want."

The inmates kept talking to me because they could see how upset I was. I told them our parents didn't know we were here. The inmates told me about a corrupt cop there, who for money, would do favors. I still had two hundred and fifty dinar on me the cop didn't find. So they called the guard over. I explained to him my parents needed to know where I was. I asked him if I gave him the money would he call them for me. At first he said no and he asked for more money. So I told him this was all I had and it would be enough to buy him a pack of cigarettes. So he said ok. He asked me for the number and said he would call. I asked him to please tell me who answered the phone at my house. This way I knew he called them. He came back a couple of hours later and he told me my brother Ayad had answered the phone. I felt so much better now. I knew my parents knew my location and we would see what happens.

For about three weeks I was detained in jail. Every day the guards would take me out and beat and torture me. Every time they took me out of the cell to take me to the interrogation room, they put the cuffs on so tight I couldn't feel my hands. They would also make you bend forward at the waist when you walked, and this would make the cuffs pinch even more. When we got to the room they would hang me upside down and kick me. They would blindfold me and punch me. The worst was when they would whip me. I cannot describe how bad it stung and I will never forget the sensation. The reason for the torture was so they could break you down and get you to confess to the crime which was written on the report. I didn't confess. I refused to die for a crime I didn't commit. My friends would not get beaten like me and I was thankful for this because they didn't deserve to be there. The report the officer wrote lied and said I was anti-government and I had attacked him. The officer's family members were the ones who carried out the interrogation torture and they all had the same last name al-Dulaimi.

There were guys in the jail who had been there for years. They had been beaten and tortured like me every day, but for years. Some of them had such scars. They had worse torture used on them. Many of them had electric shocks used on them. There was a whole underground jail too. Thank God I was in the above-ground jail. To me the underground jail was worse than death. Those men had been down there for years. They had not seen the sun or been let out to exercise their legs in decades. Many of them couldn't walk. They had diseases and bone problems. They were fed only once a day and they were so dirty and they had dried feces on them. It was a scene which would forever be burned in my mind. The worst part was most of those men had done nothing wrong to deserve to be held there. They had lost everything and they never saw their families again.

Money Persuades the Corrupt

My parents had been looking for me along with the parents of my two friends. They had located us in this jail. Thank God the guard called my parents and told them where I was because my parents and my friends' parents would never have found us. My dad and the other fathers would come and speak to the authorities at the jail every day trying to get us out. The good news was the director of the jail was as corrupted as anything and would take money to let you out. He had told my dad if he got the money he would destroy the report and let us out like nothing ever happened. He asked for a huge sum of money. It was such a high amount my whole family aunts, uncles and cousins had to contribute because my parents didn't have enough. But it had to be done. After being in jail for one month your paperwork would go to a judge named Awad Hamed al-Bandar.

Awad Hamad al-Bandar was a Revolutionary judge during Saddam Hussein's presidency. He was not someone to go in front of. He had a court room one time of one thousand people who were against the government. He split the room in half. Five hundred were ordered to be executed and the other five hundred were sentenced to go to the underground jail and never see the light of day again. After America liberated Iraq Al-Bandar was tried at the Al-Dujail Trial for crimes against humanity for issuing death sentences. He was hung to death on November 5, 2006. If my friends and I had gotten in front of this judge there was no telling what he would have done to us. I would have for sure been hung or executed. Thank God I didn't have to find out.

My parents knew they had to get me out. They got the money together and paid the corrupt director so he could lose the report. Little did I know my parents and family had been working very hard to get me out. I didn't know because they couldn't see me or talk to me.

One day it was around noon time and five to six guards came to our cell. They said, "The young students, grab your stuff and walk straight!" The reaction of the inmates around us was not good. You could see by the look on their faces they knew we were dead men walking. We were so scared. The inmates patted us on the back and told us to stay strong. As the guards were walking me out of the jail I had no idea where they were taking me. All I could think was this was my time to die. I didn't know my parents had paid for me and were waiting for me. The guards walked us straight out of the jail. I couldn't believe my eyes when I saw them. I collapsed when I had gotten to them and cried. I kept apologizing to them for what I had put them through. They were so thankful they were able to get me out and they said to me, "Let's go home." Those three words were music to my ears. My two friends were set free also after their parents paid the money too. We were all alive. Scared and beaten but alive. After this whole ordeal my father told me to always carry money and cigarettes on me, even though I didn't smoke. He also said to make sure I obeyed anything the police or Ba'ath party members wanted and to give to them whatever they wanted.

After this whole jail experience I went to go visit my grandfather. He asked me if I was ok and if I needed to talk. He explained to me my going to jail was part of the family legacy. So many family members had gone to jail or were killed because it had been written they were against the government. I happened to be the youngest one ever to go to jail. He went on to tell me Saddam's whole government was a bunch of crooks. He said Iraq used to be beautiful and wonderful before Saddam. In the 1970s they called this period of time "The Good Times." He said the government had a few issues and there were some small civil things, but nothing like today. He told me Saddam had created all this corruption and turned this country upside down. He went on to tell me something I didn't understand until years later, but he told me life was like a Ferris wheel. Sometimes you are on top and sometimes you are on the bottom. He said the Ba'ath Party and Saddam might be on top now, but at some point they will be on the bottom.

As time moved on from my jail experience I tried getting more involved in sports. I would play soccer with this one kid in my neighborhood. Soccer was huge in the Middle

East so every kid played, but I wanted to try something new. I started to talk to another one of our neighbor's kids. He was a world class Judo athlete. He was the captain for the Iraqi national team. He had explained to me he started out with wrestling and he over time switched up to Judo since the sports were similar to each other. I had never tried anything like those sports before. And, the fact I could defend myself with these new sports made them even more enticing to try. He explained to me the only problem was the dojo and wrestling center was far away. It was about an hour and one half each way. There was nothing local. So my parents and I looked into it. The summer came and I started going every day. I would leave early in the morning and I would stay and train all day. I didn't come home until the night time. It was about a two hour ride on public transportation. My dad supported me one hundred percent on this and he gave me money for the public transportation since he had to work. Nobody ever saw my face around our neighborhood. My parents were happy to see me do this because it got me away from the city and any trouble which might find me. I would practice whenever I could, even when school was back in session, and I started doing tournaments. The Judo and wrestling ended up becoming a great outlet for me. It was good for me mentally and physically. Judo built up a lot of confidence in me because I was able to defend myself and it taught me how to handle certain situations.

4

9/11

I remember one afternoon when I had gotten home from school. My mom was cooking dinner and we were talking about the day. All of a sudden we see a bunch of our neighbor's kids outside cheering. My mom and I looked at each other because we couldn't figure out why they would be cheering. I went outside, and it was all our Ba'ath Party neighbors cheering because America had gotten hit. I didn't know much about America at all at the time and I didn't understand what they meant when they said America had gotten hit. So I went back inside and put the TV on. The only channel we had was the National TV station, which was Saddam TV. The title on the TV screen was "Bin Laden and his Holy Fighters have hit the enemy." Saddam TV was giving these Holy Fighters a blessing. I saw footage of this woman at the top of a building waving her hands for help. A few seconds later it showed her jump off the building. I felt so awful watching this. This poor woman was so hopeless she jumped to her death. And I hear these bastards celebrating in the street over this and watch Saddam giving his blessing.

My mom and I we were so stunned we didn't even know what to say to each other. We kept the TV on like the rest of the world watching and trying to get more information on what had happened. America was such a faraway place at the time, but no one should ever celebrate death. At the time we began to see what type of civilization we were living in and what type of generation Saddam was cultivating. Saddam always told us since 1991 the whole world was our enemy. He had educated and brainwashed the Ba'ath party to believe this. And if someone was an idiot they would follow the stupid shit he said. If someone was educated they knew this was not proper thinking. This was the reason why since 1991 Saddam would go after any professional and educated people, and why I lost so many family members. Saddam wanted a country full of idiots who bought the shit he was selling. It was one of the most disgusting displays of human behavior I had ever seen. But you couldn't voice your opinion or how you felt about it because they would execute you. So many members of our family were so against what had happened in America. My family and I knew how it felt to be attacked and lose family members. Disasters occurred every day in Iraq. We understood the pain America was feeling, and what came out on the TV a few days later made my stomach turn even more.

Saddam would never talk about other political parties or groups on TV except his Ba'ath party. But, all of a sudden now, Saddam had become a proud ally to al-Qaeda. I heard him say one day on TV America had accused him of supporting al-Qaeda, and he was so honored to be accused of such a thing. He also said the Ba'ath party would now be supporting al-Qaeda and the extreme Islamists. A short time after this grand announcement you started seeing the extreme Islamists and Ba'athists working together. In the past you would never see a union like this. I looked at this and thought to myself, as if living under the Ba'ath party wasn't bad enough now we have to deal with the extremists. This was a union for disaster. Nothing, and I say again nothing good would come out of this.

Another year had gone by after 9/11 and I had completed high school with a science diploma. I didn't feel college was for me after high school. I had other plans in mind. But fate knew my future and you will soon see the road fate took me down and how my life turned out. These experiences I had growing up rocked me to the core. I couldn't believe how evil these people could be. The one thing I wanted more than anything else was to somehow fight back against these people. At the time I had no idea how it would happen, but I figured I would have the chance at some point.

Operation Iraqi Freedom

Weeks before the war started Saddam would come on TV and tell us we were going to war with the United States and their allies. We were all so nervous and scared. More war, more bombings and more loss of life. We didn't know what to expect. Based off of our experience from 1991 we weren't sure if the Americans were going to make it all the way to Baghdad or not. I remember the day in 2003 the war started. The war started at night with air strikes. My whole neighborhood was outside and sitting on their roofs to watch the night sky light up from rockets being shot. Even though it was war, watching the rockets fly across the sky was amazing. There were no words to describe how you felt watching it. The U.S. did not target any civilians. They were targeting only the Iraqi Military, Republican Guard and military locations. A few days after these air strikes happened the American soldiers would drop from the sky and start fighting on the ground. You could not leave your house. My mom had saved up food at home before the war started knowing there would be a period of time we wouldn't be able to leave the house. It was so amazing to watch the air strikes at night. You felt like you were in the middle of a video game. My family and I were so happy to see them. I know a lot of my neighbors weren't as happy as we were.

It took only twenty one days for the soldiers to take control of Baghdad. My brother, who was watching out our windows, told me he saw an American soldier standing outside our house. Everyone was afraid to open the door. I opened our front door with caution to peek out and see if there was a soldier standing there and sure enough there was.

I decided to go see if I could speak to him. As I walked up to him he looked at me and he stared me down.

I asked him, "Where are you from?"

He responded, "I'm from Texas," and he smiled at me like he was amused by my curiosity.

I went on to ask him, "What's your name?"

He replied back to me, "My name is Brad," and he continued to smile at me.

I asked him, "Are you American? Are you going to leave soon?"

Brad replied, "Yes, I am an American and we will be here for a while."

I asked him this question because during the Gulf War everyone thought the Americans were going to stay and help make changes, but they ended up leaving. And we all saw what disaster ensued after. So this time people were worried if they were going to stay or go.

After I was done questioning Brad I walked with him and talked to him for about 3 miles. We gave him cigarettes and chai tea. I was so excited to talk to an American. I had so many questions for him. This experience was something I thought would never happen.

The U.S. is Here

In these very early days of the war the U. S. Military was starting to establish themselves. Everything was all over the place. Saddam had been taken out of power. Saddam's administration and Ba'ath party had run out of the country and hid themselves. The old Iraqi Military, Republican Guard and police were gone too. There was no order in the country. It was messy at first. But we were free. This was unusual to us. We were no longer under Saddam's pressure.

The old administration was gone and had been dismantled so now a new administration and authority needed to be established. The first steps the U.S. took were to call all the police officers back to work to serve and protect their cities, and prevent chaos from breaking out. The U.S. did something new which Iraq had never seen before by establishing the Iraqi National Guard. This new National Guard was made up of people from local villages and towns. The advantage of recruiting local residents was their knowledge of the area and what potential threats might be there. This way those people could be the authorities in their town and surrounding area. The idea of the Iraqi National Guard was to be able to defend and protect the Iraqi people, as well as help out the police. Once the National Guard was established it was time to start establishing a new official Iraqi Army. This took place in the end of December 2003 and beginning of January 2004. In order to do this the U.S. brought in a company to start recruiting and training. The company was made up of a bunch of Vietnam Veterans. They brought the vets to the North of Iraq where there was a base ready to go and they could start training the first Iraqi division.

I would watch the Americans in Baghdad. These guys worked hard. I was impressed with how hard the Americans were working and what they were establishing. My mom and a few other women in the neighborhood would cook and make bread for the soldiers. It was customary for my mom and the other women to cook because the soldiers were our guests.

There is one story I will never forget and still makes me laugh to this day. My mom spoke no English and other women in the neighborhood didn't either. So my mom and these women would listen to the soldiers laugh and joke around as they fed them. The soldiers would joke between each other. Whenever the soldiers would say "fuck you" to each other they would laugh because it was used in a joking context. Wouldn't you know this is the one phrase my mother picked up! The ladies thought it was an endearing thing to say because of the way the soldiers said it. So as the soldiers would come over to eat some of the food or bread my mom and the other women prepared for them the soldiers would say, "Thank you!" So instead of saying, "You're welcome!"

My mom and the other women would respond back and say, "Fuck you!" They said it with a smile and in such a kind and cute way. I have never seen the soldiers laugh so hard. They couldn't eat their food they laughed so hard. Here my mom and the women had no idea what they were saying. However they thought they were saying something good because the soldiers were so amused by it. They knew my mom and the other ladies had no idea what they were saying. One soldier said to me, "If we are going to teach English this would be the best thing to start out with." It was so funny. Everyone would get a good laugh. I told my mom the meaning of what she was saying. She was so embarrassed and we got the phrase, "Your welcome" perfected.

5

The New Iraqi Army

There was information circulating a new Iraqi Army was going to be forming soon. The new army was not going to have anyone from the old regime. It was going to be a brand new army. The Americans were putting it together and they were going to give us new training, new tactics and everything we needed to establish a new Iraq. We were told the highest rank the new army would see and start with was a lieutenant colonel. When I had the chance to join the Iraqi Military at the end of 2003, I couldn't jump faster at the chance. For me it was a new challenge, a new experience, and it was my chance to get the payback for what I had been through. So being able to fight back was an amazing opportunity for me. I had never had the chance to fight back. At the time I was only seventeen years old and I decided to go to the recruiting facility. When I got there I was denied because you had to be eighteen. I was so mad. I went home and I punched and kicked some walls. I was so tired of living under such stress and torture. My family was picked on and tortured in some way every day. I was as good as and mature as someone age eighteen, and a few months shy of eighteen shouldn't have made a difference. Waiting to join the army was not an option for me. There was no way in hell I was going to let this happen. So I went home and changed my age on my Iraqi gencia. The gencia was like your citizenship ID. I went back one week later to try again and it was the same recruiter.

He said, "Hey you're back.... How can I help ya?"

I replied, "I am back to join," with a big smile on my face.

He replied back to me, "You were too young to join..."

I said, "Nope! I think you misread my age on my ID."

He looked at it and laughed. He knew how bad I wanted to join. So he said to me, "As long as you go and get your parents to sign, I can let you in."

I ran home, got my mother, brought her back and she signed for me. My family was against me going into the Iraqi Army. It was not something they wanted me to do... they looked at me and told me, "You're going to die!" I didn't care I was going to do this even if it killed me. My brother was in love and was worried about leaving his girl. I on the other hand couldn't sit and watch all the shit my family went through. Even if I died trying I was going to do what I could to beat these fuckers down who stole, killed and tortured for

53

no reason. A woman we knew lost all three of her sons to Saddam's regime and they were maybe twenty years old. At the trial against Saddam they showed a video of what they had done to one of her sons. They shackled his arms in cuffs out stretched to the sides. They put his head on a wooden block. First they pulled his tongue out of his mouth and cut it off with a knife, so he would scream and feel pain. After they put him through that they took a sword and cut his head off. What kind of sick fucks would do this? I can tell you the kind I was going to hunt down!

I was part of a generation which wanted change. We wanted freedom and I wanted to aide in this change more than anyone ever knew. I had been through so much with living in the swamp, going to jail, having my mom picked on and having family executed by the regime. I felt like it was my mission, my destiny and I was going to serve. It was my only chance to get this freedom and I would do whatever it took to get it. It was enough! I had had enough! They wished me luck and I was off.

Number 19

I was number nineteen in the new Iraqi military. Yes I was only the 19th soldier and at only seventeen years old. I wanted revenge for all the death and destruction Saddam had caused. To be in a position to fight back was going to be amazing for me. It was something I needed to do. It was our time and with the aid of the U.S. Military we were ready. Freedom for us was not free, even though the U.S. Military had come in and taken down Saddam. The Ba'ath party was still operating as a terrorist organization against the U.S. Military and us. Many of the Ba'ath party members were terrorists.

At the recruiting station we had to get onto a bus and be driven to the base to start our training. I was in the first shipment to get sent to the military base. It was a five to six hour bus ride from where I was in Baghdad. The man sitting next to me asked me why I was doing this. I was so young and he bet me I would run away after the first few days of basic training. Boy I should have put some money on the table to bet! He would have lost big!

There were three different days the new recruits were getting transported to the base and I was shipped off the first day. It was a very serious training. Most of the men who would be training us were Vietnam veterans and former Marines. There were three recruiting stations. There was one located in Baghdad, one in Mosul and one in Basra. My group of guys and the second group of guys from Baghdad made it safely. The U.S. Military made a mistake with the third group of guys from Baghdad and forgot to send a convoy to escort the bus. The bus ended up getting ambushed and everyone was killed. Everyone who wanted to join was scared after this. The number of people being recruited had decreased at the recruiting stations. People were afraid to sign-up and get killed. It was a little shaky for us at the beginning. This was the terrorist's way of fighting back and scaring people so they wouldn't join and also the reason why they started this insurgency at the recruiting stations. They wanted to place fear in our hearts and discourage possible new recruits any way they could.

A New Military United

When we got to the training base there were guys from the three different recruitment locations. They were from Baghdad, Mosul and Basra. This was done so there would be a mixed Iraqi military. Even thought we were all from different backgrounds, we all shared a common desire and we were all there to help create unity within the military. This new mixed military was made up of Kurdish, Yazidis, Shiites, Sunnis and Christians. So within each platoon there was a mix of religions and ethnicities. So, for all us new soldiers who had made it to the base, our training started and we were ready. It was a training I never expected. It was rigorous and tough. But it was amazing. Those Vietnam veterans and former Marines were phenomenal. They did a fantastic job preparing us. I felt accomplished when I finished. A couple of months after I finished my infantry training I started going through the officer's training. At this point we had another group of recruits ready to go in Baghdad and Mosul. It was at this time both recruiting stations were targeted and a car bomb went off at each one. We lost all those guys also. Starting off was not easy to say the least. Our new army was much smaller than we had anticipated. It was a little disappointing and it left us with a lot of questions. There was such worry about what if we needed more guys. We felt people were reluctant to join. It would now be a couple of months before they had enough guys to start another infantry training. As an army we had what we had. The battles started and we had to work with the soldiers we had.

After training I ended up becoming a Non Commissioned Officer (NCO), Sergeant First Class. I ended up having thirty soldiers under me. I had twelve to fifteen Kurdish, a few Yazidis, Arabs and Shiites. After training for three months and finishing the infantry school I was honored to be picked as one of the Military Police personnel. So after I was chosen to be a military police officer I was sent to Camp Taji for training. I spent about another two to three months training in the MP school. During our training at the MP school we had instructors from the U.S. Air Force who were training us to become the military police. While we were training at the MP school we had an abandoned city inside the base at Camp Taji, which was a great opportunity for us to train and gain real life experience. The Americans had great knowledge and tactics. I felt the education and training we received did prepare us for the work we had ahead of us.

My Moment

So, one day while we were training at Camp Taji we had three sharp looking U.S. Marine guys show up. We had no idea these three guys were the most elite training team from the Marine Corp. We were told these guys for the next few days were going to watch our training, and they were going to pick the top twenty guys they felt had the right stuff. Those twenty guys would become a PSD Team (Personal Security Detail Team). Every guy, all few hundred of us, wanted to get a position on this PSD team. So stakes were high, and training all of a sudden became more intense. We were all nervous, and we all had a shot. It would come down to "let the best man win." During my training, I had a team I was in charge of. During one of our training drills, as my team and I were entering a fake abandoned building I noticed a bomb in the ceiling. I pulled my team out as fast as I could. After I was finished with my training scenario I was told I had completed it successfully. After my drill one of the Marine instructors/gunnery instructors came over to me and asked my name and code number. I looked over at the team of instructors who were watching me. They opened up their note books and I could see they were taking notes. I was so excited and nervous at the same time I couldn't hold it in. I had a good day. I had proven myself, but was it enough to get onto this elite team? Everyone had a dream to be on this team and I felt like I was a step ahead.

At the end of those few days of those elite instructors watching us, our commanding officers and instructors pulled our large group together. They stated if we heard our code number being called to please step up. This large group of a few hundred men was dead silent. You could hear a pin drop. Everyone was listening to see if their number was called. They called the first 10 people. I was so nervous I could feel my heart beating so hard in my chest. A few numbers later, they called my number. I couldn't believe it. To me it was like winning the lottery. After this they took our group of twenty to a classroom.

PSD Training

The Marine Corp had a specific training area inside of the base which was for this specific PSD training. It was huge. It was three to four football fields big, and there were a bunch of scenario buildings and cars inside of it for the PSD training. These new instructors sat us down and told us this was the toughest training we will have ever received. They told us we were going to be getting hit, beaten and physically hurt. They told us they were going to train us on how to protect someone. The training was going to be both in the classroom and in the field. The classroom was the briefing and information session. The threat and possible abduction would be carried out in the field training. Their last sentence to us was, "If you don't think you can do this let us know now." This is where I met my mentor Kevin Smalling. He was a Gunnery Sergeant in the Marine Corp and the head elite instructor/advisor for the training. There were two other Marine Corp instructors from MacDill Air Force Base. His job at the time was to select twenty men from the new army and take them to PSD training. Not too long ago he told me he had no idea what to expect training us, but it was his most unexpected and exciting assignment in his twenty years as a Marine.

Here is a quote from GySGT Kevin Smalling about our PSD Team:

Initially I was sourced from Marine Forces Central Command out of MacDill Air Force Base (SOCOM) as an "Instructor / Advisor" for the New Iraqi Army. I was a Gunnery Sergeant (E-7).

Later, after several weeks of training NCOs off the New Iraqi Army at the then "semi-secret base" of Kir-Kush on the Iranian border, I was called down to the Colonels office one afternoon and told that I had a new mission from CPA down in Baghdad and had been selected to go organize, build, develop a curriculum, and be the lead Instructor/Advisor for a select cadre of Iraqi MPs for what would become the first PSD Team for the Iraqi Ministry of Defense. You guys... we had no idea what to expect and what we had been tasked with.

It was the most unexpected and exciting assignment of my 20 year career...

I selected two other Marines with CQB and Instructor experience (all three of us were MSG - Embassy Marines) to go with me and we were off to Taji to write a syllabus, put together class rooms and beg, borrow or steal weapons ranges to get Hamody and the rest of the new team up to an acceptable standard for PSD work.

After we produced the new PSD Team, I was then selected to go set up the physical security of the actual Ministry of Defense Head Quarters building on the edge of the Green Zone. A US Army SFC and I were paired together for this task.

In doing all this I was working and living side by side with some of the then-relatively unknown PMC's (Private Military Contractors) which were just emerging into the public's eye.

Shortly before I left I was given a business card by an acquaintance and told I had an immediate job if I wanted it after I returned stateside and processed out of the Corps.

I swore Iraq would be the last place on earth I would ever want to see again, but as fate would have it, three months later I was back. But THAT is a different and more complex story...

GySGT Kevin Smalling

(Our PSD team inspired and impressed Kevin Smalling in so many ways. We, especially I, never realized how much we touched the Americans as well until I decided to write this book and people came out to tell me how much they wanted to be a part of this and how much I inspired them.)

Please enjoy another quote from GySGT Kevin Smalling:

Hamody had the biggest smile.

We initially thought there was something wrong with him because he couldn't quit smiling all the time when we were in the classroom. I finally pulled one of the senior guys who spoke a little English aside and, combined with our interpreter, asked him if the young kid (Hamody) was OK. He explained to us that Hamody was so excited and honored to be a part of these selected few to receive the specialized training and work with the Marines that he simply couldn't control his happiness or smiling. It was an infectious and genuine smile that he still has to this day-ask anyone who has met or knows him to describe him and I guarantee you one of the first things they will mention is his smile.

PSD Team

Our barracks and training areas were located in a secluded closed off section of Taji just North of Baghdad. We had never met Iraqis this big. I mean they were physically big guys. One had hands the size of a bunch of bananas sitting on the shelves in the produce section of a grocery store.

Most were physically big and very dignified looking men.

On the few occasions we were able to venture on to the main side of the base where all the American Military lived and worked, we went to the Chow Hall, or DFAC as the Army called it. They were rock stars when we went in - everybody wanted a picture with them. We all sat together when we ate-the Marines and this small team of Iraqi soldiers-we were all the same. I think it meant a lot to them that we genuinely felt them equal and displayed that to our fellow Americans. *On a side note:

they had to be blown away by all the food choices in that DFAC-hell, we were. Here are the Americans thousands of miles away from home on the other side of the earth, in the middle of a desert, and they can materialize fresh shrimp, steak, prime rib, and lobster-not to mention ice cubes and dessert. I have never seen as many men go back for seconds. *(Say what you will about KBR, but it was pretty damn impressive even to us.)

At the end of our course, the PSD Team held an informal formation with me and presented me with the nickname of "Saif ", Arabic for Sword. I was very flattered to be given this title and later had a patch made in Arabic that I wore on my web gear after I got out of the Corps and was employed by Dynacorp. *No one except the interpreters and the Iraqis knew what it meant so it was a tongue in cheek secret laugh to myself!

During our daily operations and training they would look at us sometimes as if they were wondering why we carried ourselves the way we did, what we were thinking, how we felt about being there assigned to help them. They were very proud to be training with us and were soaking up everything we were putting out, including some of our lingo...

I set aside time after training about once every three days for us to just sit and talk as men. We would talk about anything and everything. I thought it was important to present ourselves in the right way, and just as importantly, to let them know that we were genuinely interested and respected what they had to say and think.

They had questions about us, about America, (was it really like in the movies?) our homes, where we were from, what it was like there, and ALL thanked us for coming to help them. Some asked the most unexpected and touching questions: "How is your family?" "Is your sister, wife, son, or daughter OK?" "Do you miss them?" They were genuinely concerned about our feelings of missing our families and loved ones.

It seemed to be unthinkable to them that we were so far away from our homes for such long periods of time, and that we volunteered to do it. *(It is a little unthinkable now looking back on it.) So many sacrifices....

*(It's surprising what Americans take for granted. I never had any problems with any of the things I saw or did in the line of duty, but I'll say the closest I ever came to a "breakdown" was when I returned stateside and went into a Wal-Mart. I was so overwhelmed by the choices and amounts of everything that I had to turn around and walk out and wrap my head around it for a bit.)

If they were in awe of us and proud to be receiving training from an elite team of U.S. Marines, we were all personally rewarded by knowing at the end of it all we contributed to something good in a chapter of history.

The Iraqis reminded me of Italians-family was the center of life.

Most Iraqis weren't bad people at all. They had no illusions or dreams of grandeur, or unattainable dreams of becoming millionaires. What was important to Iraqis were their families.

Iraqis simply wanted to work, come home to their families, eat dinner with their families, be together with their families and live safe lives.

Family was the most important thing to them.

GySGT Kevin Smalling

The training started and after the first day, one guy quit. The next day I was called over by one of the Marine Corp instructors. We called this guy the mean guy. He gave me a person to protect. He told me, "You protect this person at all costs." I walked over to the person I was going to protect and before I knew it, this Marine Corp instructor attacked me. He was twice my size, remember I was only eighteen, and he jumped on top of me and beat the shit out of me. It was at this moment I realized these instructors wanted the training to be real. He punched me in the stomach, he grabbed me and threw me on the ground and he pulled me on the gravel. After he grabbed the person I was trying to protect. I was sitting on the ground, knees bleeding and he bent over spitting on me as he yelled at me and said "If you're going to protect someone you better die protecting them before someone gets to them." The whole team felt at the time this was going to be a tough qualification and training.

The next day each one of us received a hand gun, a Walther P99 and two magazines. All of us were nervous now that we had a hand gun. We had also received a knife and were told we were going to do knife training with the instructors. These instructors scared the shit out of us, as a team, and we had no idea what the hell to expect. From this day forward the training intensified and we were in the range shooting every day. Our hand speeds were not fast enough. We were nowhere near the hand speed of the instructors. The training was so intense to the point we weren't even given a break. We started driving and I had never driven before. Kevin Smalling was the person who taught me how to drive. You can only imagine how this experience was. I was nervous with these drills. I had to protect someone and try to pretend I knew how to drive at the same time. I was so afraid I was going to hit a building or a wall. The buildings were close together and the walls were right next to them. You had to drive at top speeds and slam on your brakes to get the person you were protecting in your car to the next vehicle.

During this rigorous training our group went down from twenty guys to seventeen. People had a hard time surviving this training. It was a bigger challenged than any of us thought. But I knew I couldn't drop out. I would have disappointed the shit out of myself and my reasons for being there.

Range Attack

One day we were at the shooting range. The range was located right at the border of the base. We had a very tough challenge in which we had to shoot at two different targets and switch magazines while doing this. Each magazine only had two bullets in it and each bullet had to hit the target. After you shot your two bullets at the target, you had to drop the used magazine, insert the new magazine, turn to the new target in the opposite direction, gain your sight again fast and shoot the next two bullets at the new target. And, it is all being timed by the instructors. The whole team had a hard time hitting the second target. I was the last person in the line to shoot. All of a sudden I hit the first target with both my bullets. On the second target only one of my bullets hit the target. But, this meant I passed the drill and training. I was the only guy to hit the second target.

After the drill and for the rest of the day we were doing more shooting and practicing. All of a sudden we see bullets start flying over our head from behind the hill we were shooting at. Was this another drill where now we were being shot at? The Marine SGT, who was the instructor next to me, grabbed me as I was shooting and threw me to the side of the range which had a sand pit so I would be protected. I had no idea what the hell was going on. This was the first time I had a bullet fly over my head. I realized my instructor had saved my life. If I had been standing up a few seconds longer I would have been hit in the head by a bullet and killed. Those Instructors had our PSD team covered and protected in no time. They threw all of us down into a sand pit so we wouldn't be hit by a bullet. One of the instructors even threw his body over the top of all of us to protect us. The PSD team and I after this had such immense respect for the Marines. They put their lives on the line to protect us without hesitation and let me tell you there were only a few of them, 17 of us and who knew how many shooting at us, but they took position and protected us in an instant.

My mentor Kevin Smalling wrote this about this range attack:

The attack while at the Weapons Range in Taji happened while we were fine tuning the shooting skills of the PSD teams with their side arms. We had been issued brand new Walther P99's.

Surprisingly, almost all of the Iraqis were decent shots and had no bad fundamental shooting habits to break. They just needed to be trained on when not to shoot more so than when to shoot.

Our barracks and ranges were on the North Eastern most side of Taji and we routinely took fire and incoming from the little island created by the Tigris directly to our East.

*Side note - when we initially broke out the pistols everything got real quiet. We didn't know it until later but in the past when Saddam or some of his thugs whipped out a pistol it was when they were going to execute someone. It left an impact if not by personal experience by frightening stories. Either way, it certainly had a lasting effect on them. As an example, one afternoon while in our barracks, myself and a few of the others had responded to a riot at the regular New Iraqi Army barracks several hundred yards away from ours (the Iraqi PSD boys lived away from everyone else in a secluded barracks.) The riot revolved around some of the Baghdad central boys singling out a fellow soldier because he was Kurdish and were in the process

of beating the shit out of him along with throwing stones at his head. A few had hit their mark. I was in the bed of a small truck as we came to halt next to him and jumped out to stop the violence. I was carrying a HK MP5 along with the Walther strapped to my thigh. They weren't too distracted from accomplishing their mission or taking too much notice when I was yelling at them to get back and stop until I un-holstered the pistol-then they all quickly ran back inside their barracks.

We were in the middle of a course of fire when heavy weapons fire starting hitting close to us. One of the other two Marine Instructors assigned with me grabbed all the PSD guys and put them in a vehicle service trench (think Oil change pit) while myself and the other Staff Sergeant (SSgt) grabbed out gear and headed to the berm of the range to identify the source and return fire. About half way to the top of the berm several Katyusha rockets hit close to our position.

Once to the top of the Berm we saw a truck about three hundred yards out with what looked like improvised rocket launchers on its bed. They began throwing them off into the reeds of the field and were driving off.

*I got on the radio to the OPS TOC and transmitted that we were in taking fire. *(The Ops Center / TOC that controlled the weapons Ranges we were using. This is where we called in our range times (Hot/Cold.)*

To our advantage, Taji was a base where some U.S. Rotary Wing assets were based so it only took them a couple of minutes to respond.

OPS relayed our situation over to the Air Cav Quick Reaction Force (QRF) and they dispatched a couple of Kiowa's almost immediately to our Range. One of the Marines stayed hunkered down with the Iraqis while I and the other SSgt got on the edge of the berm and relayed description and position of the truck and bad guys. The Kiowa was directly above us as I called in the position distances and descriptions over the radio.

The truck and its occupants were later apprehended by some ground forces just outside of Taji base.

At the end of it the Iraqi PSD boys were safe, and we were safe.

We returned to the range the next morning and continued our training.

Another day in Iraq.

We were put in for Combat Action Ribbons but the Iraqis were never awarded.

GySGT Kevin Smalling

The Rock

I met the twenty most interesting guys I had ever met in my life at PSD training. The first day there with them I had no idea I would be friends with them for the rest of my life. I was the youngest of the bunch. There was one man in his 40s. He didn't speak much. We nicknamed him "The Rock." We nicknamed him this because he didn't speak, he never cracked a smile, he showed no emotion and he had scars on his face and body. Looking at those scars I always thought they must have some story to tell. My friends said he looked beaten up like a rock! I wanted to ask him what those scars were from but I was kind of afraid to. The training was hard. So hard! I had never worked so hard in my life. I was beaten up but I loved it and if this is what it took to fight back I would do it all day and night. I would watch this guy train and he made the training look like nothing. He had so much anger inside of him it fueled him. This guy had to be more than twice my age and what shape he was in.

So one day I had "The Rock" as my partner. He asked me, "What's your name?"

I replied, "Hamody!" I was shocked I never heard him speak before.

He said to me, "I had a son years ago, you look like you would be his same age, but I lost him."

I didn't understand, I asked him, "How did you lose him?"

He said, "I lost him and my wife. They were taken from me by the government years ago and they are gone forever." He went on to ask me "You are so young, why are you here? You are too young to die!"

I was a little offended. I replied, "No I'm not! I'm here to get these bastards and free my family." I asked him "What's your name?"

He replied, "My name is Khalid." And he smirked after he answered me.

I later in the PSD training got to know Khalid very well and I was the only one he talked with. He had a lot of pain inside of him. You could see it in his face. He was there to fight for revenge too. One of the PSD guys got sick. Khalid went over to check on him. He looked at him and explained to an American medic what he needed for the sick PSD guy. None of us understood how he knew so much about medicine and the American medic looked surprised too. So now he had to tell me his story!

I asked him, "How do you know what's wrong with him? Are you a doctor?"

Khalid responded, "I was a surgeon." He was a medical doctor and professor at a medical college in Iraq and he taught surgery.

The Regime back in the day targeted a lot of professors because many of them were against the regime and the government. The professors were very smart people and knew the government was no good. The regime captured Khalid, his wife and son. He was thrown in one of Saddam's underground jails, which was worse than death by execution because prisoners would be tortured to death. His wife and son were killed and their bodies thrown into chemicals which dissolved their bodies. This had happened back in the mid 1980s. He was released from the underground prison a few years prior to joining the new Iraqi army. He had so much hate against Saddam and the government he wanted to kill them all and after that he wanted nothing more than to die also. My heart went out to this guy. The scars on his face were from being beaten every day in the jail and from the electric shock torture. When I would train I would do thirty to forty push-ups. When Khalid trained the anger he had inside of him would come out and he would be able to do one hundred push-ups in the same amount of time.

The regime jails and the underground jails were nothing but torture chambers. Saddam had the most barbaric torture procedures. I remember one of my PSD guys telling me, prisoners naked would have to sit on the neck of a bottle and more times than not those bottles would break and the broken glass would rip the men up inside their rectum. Many of them had such colon and rectum problems. Men would also get electrocuted, have chemicals thrown on them and some would get hung upside down and have their heads beaten. When the Americans came in and freed an above ground prison, they heard banging in the floor. Special Forces were brought in to investigate and more underground jails had been discovered. The men had not been fed for a few days after the American's came in and they were banging things against the bars to get attention because they were hungry. As the men were freed some of them asked if the Iran-Iraq war was still going on. Most of them had not seen the sun in decades. Humanitarian groups had to come in and help these men acclimate back to the outdoors and life. They needed physical therapy and nutritional therapy. The guards had done a number on these poor guys. It was terrible and inhumane. I was so nervous about making my first kill. I couldn't imagine having to kill someone living and breathing in front of me. But, the more I heard these stories and saw what these bastards did, I felt like the first kill might be a lot easier than I thought.

When we finished PSD training Khalid went out on every mission. He never slept. He went out on every raid, even if it was a suicide mission he was the first one ready to go. He would never let me walk into a building first. He always wanted to go first. He wanted to kill anyone he could and then after he wanted to die. He wanted to see his wife and son again. He couldn't wait to be reunited with them. He had no other family and there would be no one to claim him when he died. All the elders in his family had passed on. Khalid and I developed a very good friendship. He confided a lot in me, as I did him. I think he felt close to me because I reminded him of his son because I was so young.

He made me promise to bury him in a certain spot when he ended up getting killed in action. He had a place picked out in a national park where there would be a lot of families and children running around him. He wanted to be placed where there was nothing but happiness and children laughing and enjoying themselves. No one would be allowed to be buried there but this is where Khalid wanted to rest. Because he had endured such hardship and torture he wanted to be laid to rest in a place where there was nothing but happiness.

One night during a raid which lead into a heavy fire fight, Khalid was the first one to go in and he was shot multiple times. I didn't go on the mission he went on. I was woken up around 2 a.m. The team called me and told me he had passed. So we got into the truck and grabbed a few shovels. We told the park ranger we had official business in the park and we got past the gate. The guys and I buried him around 4 a.m. We had to get him buried fast because the sun was coming up, it was in the middle of the park and we didn't want anyone to see us. His body didn't even go to the morgue. I wanted to make sure Khalid made it to his final resting place. He had no one else in this world and at this particular spot he would be at peace. I could take you today and show you where he is, but promised him I would never tell anyone where he was. It's my promise and secret for him and I will take this secret to my grave. I know he is with his family and even in death he is right where he wanted to be.

Khalid told me one night before he died that even when he was gone he would always have my back. He said he would never leave this fight. I used to laugh and tell him we'll see. I have to say he kept his promise. There were so many times while fighting I was in some tough situations. I would sometime feel this would be the day I met God. But, I always made it through. I don't know how I made it out but I always felt he had my back.

I told you about Khalid now because he was such a good friend to me. Even though he didn't pass until January 2005 I wanted to dedicate a section in my book to him. I had lost a couple of good friends of mine the first year in combat from 2004-2005.   His life story always got to me and always stayed with me. It meant so much to me to make sure I placed him where he wanted to rest. So even though this story seems a little out of place I wanted to make sure his story lived on and since we met at PSD training I felt it was the appropriate place to put his story.

After finishing PSD training my first reality of being on the front line and being at war was in Fallujah in 2004. Everybody in the Iraqi army went to fight here. It was the biggest threat and the toughest fight at the time. We had trained up near the Iranian borders and we went straight from there to Fallujah. Fallujah was the first place the Americans had gotten hit. The Americans were in other cities in Iraq, but this is where the first American HMMWV was hit by an RPG (Rocket Propelled Grenade). The RPG happened to be shot by Saddam's Al Fedayeen. The Al Fedayeen was Saddam's most loyal suicide fighters. The battles which ensued there had us fighting both al-Qaeda and members from Saddam's Ba'ath party. This was due to the fact Saddam had created this union between al-Qaeda and his Ba'athists back after 9/11. This is why the battles in Fallujah were always so much tougher. Because both groups were together fighting against the Americans. In Fallujah there was the U.S. Army and some of the Iraqi National Guard. Many of the Iraqi National Guard had been killed because they did not have the proper training or the proper tactics to fight at this level. We were the first Iraqi military on the ground. We had to go in to support the Army and the Marines who were there and get al-Qaeda out of Fallujah.

My wishes had come true. If there was anyone more ready to fight these bastards, I was ready as well as Khalid and the rest of our PSD team. It was our wish coming true of starting to fight back for freedom and getting these bastards who tortured us for so long. We got in there and fought. For me this was the first time I ever got to hold a gun against the people who always put me and my family through hard times. It felt great and we did it. We were engaging in clashes and fire fights with the local tribes. Once all the citizens of Fallujah left and evacuated the area we started to patrol neighborhoods. We would go from house to house clearing buildings. Over time we had pushed the local terrorists out and Fallujah calmed down for a little bit. Together with the Marines, our trained Iraqi army and PSD team we gained control of Fallujah. After Fallujah we were pulled back to Baghdad with the MP. We were supposed to go to Baghdad from the beginning but Fallujah needed us there more. Over time foreign fighters started to come into Fallujah creating more problems and battles for the Marines.

After Fallujah my PSD team and I were sent back to our basic positions within our own platoons. Our PSD team would come together when there were special missions, a raid or a particular person who needed to be detained.

Upon leaving Fallujah I was pulled with the MP down to Haifa Street. Haifa Street was a place in Baghdad full of terrorists and terrorism, and we had big problems there. The group of soldiers there were over whelmed and our help was needed right away. So I was off to Haifa Street.

6

Haifa Street Battle

We were pulled down to Haifa Street because there was a recruiting station there for the new Iraqi Military. The new recruits upon leaving the recruiting center kept getting killed by the terrorists. On Haifa Street there were a lot of old Syrian Ba'ath Party refugees who used to be supported by Saddam. Also there was an apartment building which housed many ex-Iraqi Republican Guard members, ex-Iraqi military intelligence officers and members of the old regime. So we were up against Ba'ath party members, terrorists and Saddam supports. These guys had extensive military training, weapons, money and support. Later on, this is the group of people would become the Islamic State.

So, at this point, three brigades were being left behind in Fallujah to keep order. My brigade was the only brigade sent to Haifa Street in Baghdad to aid in the situation. My brigade was broken up into three battalions. One battalion was sent to the Ministry of Defense (MOD), another battalion, which was my battalion, had to go to the Haifa Street base and the last battalion protected the recruiting station, which was attached to our Haifa Street military base. The buildings on Haifa Street were big tall buildings, many stories high, with a lot of opportunity for terrorists to hide. Imagine going to Times Square with all those tall buildings trying to fight terrorists. Going into this assignment we knew it was going to be pure street fighting. It was not going to be like Fallujah. With the power and weapons the opposing forces had they were more capable then the terrorists we had fought against in Fallujah, and more capable than our military.

Haifa Street was only a two mile long street. It was the longest and deadliest two miles anyone could imagine. Haifa Street was one of the most dangerous streets in the world.

The Hardest Day

Haifa Street, now looking back on it, ended up being one of my most difficult and saddest missions. I was there to protect the recruiting station so young men could come and join the Iraqi army without being compromised on their way there. We had to fight against terrorists and watch out for car bombs. It was not an easy job. The Americans were there helping us too, but snipers and car bombs took its toll on us. Both our military and the Americans got their asses kicked daily on Haifa Street. The terrorists were brutal and many Americans and Iraqis lost their lives there. The IEDs the

82

terrorists left on Haifa Street were so strong they could destroy an American Bradley (a heavy armored vehicle). It was brutal and deadly every day.

The bus drivers who drove the public transportation vehicles for people to get around the city were working with the terrorists. They had deals with the terrorists to take the new recruits who had just signed with the Iraqi military to the end of Haifa Street. This way the terrorists could pick them up and execute them. So for me, my military life and everything good or bad which came out of it, started at this point.

I had to patrol Haifa Street every once in a while. As a platoon leader my Commander relied on me often. I spoke English, I had no problems communicating with the Americans and I was always sent out first. One day I was called up to my Commander's office and he explained to me we had a big problem. There was an intelligence source which had informed him many new recruits had been executed on Haifa Street and their bodies were thrown all over the place under the bridge. This bridge was a bridge which Haifa Street ran on and it went over the Tigris River. I was ordered to take my platoon to go get those bodies and take them to the hospital so their families could pick them up. As my platoon and I went to go get the bodies there were twenty seven of us.

So we started to drive up Haifa Street and something didn't look right. It was in the middle of the afternoon and

not many vehicles or people were around. It was deserted.
Haifa Street was a very busy area with restaurants and
stores. There was always a lot going on there. I was there for
a job and I had to go get those bodies, but it felt like
something was about to happen. The air didn't feel right. The
plan by the terrorists was, after we drove down Haifa Street,
they were going to plant a lot of IEDs (Improvised Explosive
Device) on the street behind us, so after they surrounded us
and we called our Quick Reaction Force (QRF) to come in
and help us, the QRF would get blown up and we would be
captured. The soldiers would be hung alive and killed. Their
overall plan was to discourage people from joining the new
army.

And Then There Were 9

My team and I had made it safely to the underside of
the bridge. Under the bridge there was a small playground
for children, bridge barriers and park benches. It was a nice
playground and park for families which over looked the
Tigris River. As we started to walk away from the trucks we
were driving, which were regular Nissan pick-ups and not
armored vehicles, those trucks started getting hit with RPGs.
My gunners and drivers were all killed by those RPGs.
Thankfully the other soldiers who were with me had left the

trucks and had taken the heavy machine guns with them. I lost 8 soldiers within the first couple minutes of being there. My soldiers and I all took positions like something was going to happen. I had to somehow get to the dead bodies and make sure they did not have bombs inside of them. I couldn't risk losing more of my soldiers. As soon as I looked over and touched the bodies I could see the bodies were fresh and still bleeding. These young men had just been killed within the last hour or so and no one was alive.

From the buildings above us we had snipers shooting at us, machine guns and RPGs coming at us. There were terrorists hiding in the trees about one hundred feet from us. The first thing we had to do was take a position and taking a position was not easy. Some of the soldiers took position behind the playground and some took position behind the bridge barriers. The barriers were big and strong and those barriers protected us from the RPGs being shot at us. The battle went on from about 3:00 pm until about 6:00 pm, which was when the Americans were finally able to get there and help us under the bridge. We did have a QRF and I did call on them to come help us, but the fighting was so intense the QRF could not get to us. During all the fire exchange I didn't hear the explosions on the bridge above me. But the IEDs which were planted had gotten my QRF. Were they alive or all dead? I didn't know. We were stuck behind the barrier. If you tried to jump into the river to swim, there was a sniper on top of the building who would shoot at you. I did lose one soldier who tried to swim to get away. I had heard from other soldiers my platoon leader had run out of ammunition and he surrendered. So they got him too. I was left to lead the platoon in this battle.

All of a sudden I hear a strange voice come over my radio. I had realized at the moment and it was confirmation for me that the terrorists had gotten my platoon leader. I heard screaming in the back ground, and it was my QRF screaming for help. The QRF, who was on their way to help me and my soldiers, had been ambushed on their way to us and the few QRF members who were still alive had turned around and went back to the base. There was a large number of terrorists and we were a small platoon. The terrorists were well coordinated and had been planning this for a long time. I was so devastated. I couldn't let my soldiers know what had happened to our QRF. The terrorists had started to communicate with me through the radio they took from my platoon leader. I tried to get around to take all the radios away from the squad leaders. I got the radios and threw them in the water. I did this because if they heard what was going on they would have surrendered on me. If they ended up surrendering I wouldn't be writing this story today. I kept my radio close so I could figure out how the hell I was going to get us out of this. The only people to get me out of this now would be the Americans. The Americans were on their way to come help us. They had seen what happened to my QRF, so they had to turn around and come from the other side of the bridge to attack. We had to continue fighting until they got there, which took time. The terrorists over the radio told me my QRF was destroyed and to surrender. They told me if we put our weapons down and they would let us go. I knew what they were saying was a lie and this was the exact reason why I threw the other radios away. I didn't want my soldiers to hear this and surrender. I wanted to keep morale up as best I could and continue fighting for our lives until the Americans came. One of my soldiers saw me throwing the radios in the water and asked me why I was throwing the radios away after taking the batteries out of them. I told him the radios were dead and to keep fighting because the QRF was coming.

The voice on the radio was an Iraqi voice. It turned out later the voice ended up being one of Saddam's highest trained military leaders. His name was Colonel Hachem, based on his previous Iraqi Military rank. He was from the old military and he ended up being one of the biggest terrorists in Baghdad and took many American lives until the day he was captured. He was working for the Islamic State at this time for Abu Musab al-Zarqawi. Zarqawi was the leader of al-Qaeda in Iraq, which at the time they called themselves the Islamic State in Iraq. Hachem was captured in 2005 by the Americans.

Once I started talking with Hachem on the radio I had to fuck with him over the radio. I couldn't let him know he was getting to me. So, I told him I was coming for him very soon and when I got to him I was going to go fuck his sister. He got pissed off and the fire fight got worse. During this time my best squad leader and best friend, Yehia, who trained with me at PSD training was hit. He was covering for other soldiers who had been shot. He would go out and drag them back behind the barriers for protection. He ended up getting shot himself. The bullet went in one side of him and out the other. I had to go out and get him. My Kurdish soldiers covered me well with heavy guns so I could grab him. The Kurdish knew how to defend and fight after fighting against Saddam for years. I got to him in time before his last breaths and he looked at me. Yehia's last words to me were "The bastards got me. Promise me you will not let them walk away."

I told him I would never let them walk away. I was crushed and my heart was in my throat. I ordered a cease fire with my soldiers, so we wouldn't run out of ammunition.

I told my soldiers "If you see it, shoot it, if nothing hold your fire, were going to be here for a while!"

My soldiers kept asking me, "Where's the QRF?"

I didn't know what to say. As a group we kept together. I looked around and I only had seven to eight soldiers who were still able to fight. I was trying to figure out where everyone had gone and it was at that moment I realized how many soldiers I had lost. I was also shot in the leg myself but I didn't even realize it. I took a bullet out of my magazine, put it in my left shirt pocket. This bullet was going into my head when the terrorists got to us. I was not going to let them take me alive.

The fire fight continued on and off. I was out of hope. I knew today would be my last day. We had been defeated. We were tired, shot, thirsty, and covered in our brothers blood. My guys kept asking me about the QRF and I told them the QRF is on their way to us. The terrorists had gotten the bodies of my gunners and drivers and put them in a pile and set them on fire. It was the hardest thing to watch your soldiers burning, knowing this was going to happen to you next.

As I sat there I made up my mind we were going to get the hell out of there. I was down to sixteen bullets left. All of a sudden heavy gun fire started to hit the building in front of me where the terrorists were. The gun fire was coming from behind me. I looked and there was an Apache flying over the river and it was engaged and shooting at the building. Tanks were also there shooting. So the Apache and tanks were able to stop the terrorists from firing. The Americans made it down the bridge to me and the military ambulances were right behind. Twenty-seven soldiers, including myself, went out to retrieve those bodies and only nine of us came back. Eighteen soldiers were taken from me and my platoon. I still did not know how many guys we lost up above on the bridge. We were devastated, but I was lucky to be alive and determined. We weren't sure how this new Iraqi army was going to turn out because we couldn't defend ourselves. Our army kept getting slaughtered.

Many of our higher officials were killed in this battle. The terrorists in the evening celebrated on Haifa Street so we could see them. They celebrated because they had defeated the Iraqi army. They took the uniform of my lieutenant, after they had captured him and beheaded him, and hung it up on Haifa Street for all to see. They wanted to show us they could defeat us and bring our morale down. They may have gotten me down today, but I was for damn sure they would never get me or my men again.

I had spoken to Yehia's father when he came to pick up Yehia's body. I found out his wife was pregnant. I felt so bad because this baby would never know his father. Yehia ended up having a son and he will be turning ten this year. I always did my best to keep up with as many families as I could. I wanted to make sure their families ended up being okay and life had moved on for them.

July 29, 2004, two days after my battle on Haifa Street, we had finished burying our dead from the previous battle. My Iraqi Commander and I decided something big had to happen to get these guys on Haifa Street. We invited everyone we could to help us with this battle. Over seven thousand troops, both the American First Calvary Division and Iraqi Military, gathered together to get revenge on these bastards who had taken so many of our brothers and sisters. We invited Iraqi Military units from all over the country to send squads to participate in this battle. We entered Haifa Street with no armored vehicles at all. We came in from four different directions so the terrorists couldn't run. The terrorists decided not to fight us. The terrorists hid instead. It was hard telling who was who, but based on intelligence information we were able to capture a huge number of terrorists. Around thirty high profile terrorists were captured. It was an amazing effort to show they had not beaten us. We were still there and ready to fight. No bullets were shot on Haifa Street.

7

Battlefield Promotion

It was after the horrific battle on Haifa Street I got my battlefield promotion to Sergeant Major. I was the youngest Sergeant Major ever in the history of the Iraqi Army. This is a promotion for someone thirty years older than me. But, because our Iraqi army was only one division and a few National Guard units, there were not many non-commissioned officers or soldiers left. My lieutenant was killed in the Haifa Street battle leaving me to lead the battle there for a couple of hours. There were older non-commissioned officers from the old Iraqi Army but they were not courageous enough to lead this new developing army. They also did not have the physical capabilities to take the stress of the front line. They were better off working in administration. My Commander felt I was capable enough to handle a promotion like this and I had the skills to communicate with our soldiers, fix our battalion and get morale up. From here my journey would start, not knowing the events which would transpire in the next couple of years.

I was excited and afraid at the same time to have such a high promotion bestowed on me at such a young age. Many Americans would meet me and be shocked at how young I was. I got to meet and work with many great high ranking officials in the American military. I had a lot of people who wanted to meet with me because they couldn't believe how young I was. It was a wonderful honor to be placed at this rank. However, I lost so many people who I cared about I would have given up the promotion in a second to have them back in my life. I had a lot of respect from my soldiers because they knew Haifa Street was the battle I had gone through. With this rank in the Iraqi Military, I had to be one of the first guys at the front of the battle while the commanders stayed back.

I had only one year in the military. Because I spoke English it was a bonus, and I was able to communicate with the Americans much easier than most Iraqi military officials. Little did I know speaking English would put me in the crossfire of some corrupt Iraqi Generals and Colonels!

Ministry of Defense

After being stationed at Haifa Street and the recruiting center, because of my new promotion, I was stationed at the Ministry of Defense (MOD) in Baghdad. The Iraqi military needed new leadership there and my Commander sent me. There were a lot of sensitive people, both Iraqi military and American walking into the MOD, such as generals, colonels and other high ranking officials. The MNSTC-I (Multi-National Security Transition Command- Iraq) was located right next to the MOD and there were a lot of big American officials there such as General Martin Dempsey and General David Petraeus. The MNSTC-I was like the headquarters for NATO. All the top military officials from around the world who were working with the Iraqis were there. The MNSTC-I was in the green zone and the MOD was in the red zone, but it was only meters which separated the two areas. The check point for the MOD, which is where I was, was located near Check Point 1 for the MNSTC-I and the green zone. It was where the red zone and green zone met up. Because of all the sensitive people there my PSD team was sent to the MOD to provide security in all the different departments inside the MOD. The PSD team was back working together minus a couple of those who had died like Khalid and Yehia.

I was told when I joined the Iraqi army in 2003 since we were a new army there would be no rank higher than a lieutenant colonel. So when I got the MOD I was surprised to see there were Iraqi Generals.

The Old Boys are back

The US Government seemed to have different goals which didn't coincide with what was presented to us in 2003 and 2004. There was a law implemented by the new government and the U.S. which stated no Ba'ath party or Regime members could come back and hold positions. So, I got concerned because I started to see a lot of old Iraqi army members coming back. It's not because they were from the old army, but because there were many corrupt ones and I couldn't understand what prompted bringing these individuals back. It was one of those "what the fuck" moments. Once I saw these guys coming back I felt like the U.S. might not have the best background information on these guys. Me and the rest of my men, we were the new army. We knew our agenda of fighting for freedom and making Iraq a better place. Why were these old generals and military members back and what was their agenda? A lot of them worked for Saddam and were very loyal to him and his regime. Could these people be trusted? Or are they coming to the new army to destroy it? To date I have no idea what decisions were made to bring these guys back or how they even got there. I am not sure who made the decision to bring these guys back. Was it the Ambassador at the time Paul

Bremmer? Or whom? I found out later Bremmer appointed Ahmed Chalabi to take over the government from him. Once Chalabi was appointed he started appointing people to his government positions and Mohan happened to be one of them because he was a Shiite. These appointments by Chalabi brought back a lot of corrupt members and terrorists.

Mohan

I was surprised to see General Mohan at the MOD as a two star general, a major general. Back in the day, if you remember, I told you General Mohan was an Iraqi general who participated in the 1991 killings of the rebels who were fighting against Saddam and the Ba'athist party. Mohan was a Shiite. He was not a Sunni, but he was a tried and true member of the Ba'athist party. He was also a member of the Iraqi intelligence service. He had gone to military school in Bulgaria and Russia. He spoke Russian. He was trained by the Russians and he was a professional intelligence officer. He claimed Saddam had put him in jail as a political prisoner. Come to find out he did go to jail, but not as a political prisoner. He had gotten drunk one night and he made a joke about Saddam. Because of the joke he was thrown in jail for eight months. After his time in jail he was put back to work. The question for me was, was he back in the Army for the anti-Saddam movement or was he here for other motivations. We were confused and Mohan had become the leader in the Operations center. He had control over all the operations and all the information going in and out of there.

There were American advisors who worked in the operations center to see how the Iraqis were operating. From the look on General Mohan's face and a few others faces in the department you could tell they hated having the Americans around and they looked at me and my men like we were the enemy. Like we were the rebels and the anti-government people from back in the day. You could see we were not welcomed at all.

There were a lot of these old Iraqi military guys who had shown back up. The MOD had numerous departments such as logistics, communications, supplies, transportation and everything else which makes up a military. I don't know if the job of rebuilding was made easier by bringing these guys back but many of them were the wrong guys to bring back. Just because they had past military experience didn't mean they were the ones for the job.

General Mohan had his own political party outside of the MOD. This was a political group made up of ex-Iraqi military officers. They had meetings outside of the MOD and they all worked together inside the MOD. It was like they were coming back to take control of the Iraqi Army. Mohan would support the officers in his political party and try to get them into different sensitive positions so they could have control over the military. Over time the Americans started to look into General Mohan. His stories seemed suspect and the U.S. Military ended up freezing his position for a while. He was not allowed to get involved in sensitive situations. The Americans had him sit at his desk and do small tasks.

My American Friends

At the MOD I loved the communication with the Americans and the experience for me was unbelievable. The MOD was an old parliament building from Saddam's time and it was staffed by Iraqis, but there was an American advisor in every department. These American advisors would come to the MOD during the day and work, and after hours they would go back to the MNSTC-I. The old MOD was destroyed and this new MOD was huge. You could walk miles inside of it. It was five stories high and it had a basement. The floors were long and doors were made out of metal. I was in charge of all security both inside and outside the MOD. If anything went down in the MOD it was my ass on the line. Now with all these old military and regime characters starting to surface it was going to make my job more of a challenge. It was my responsibility to protect all Americans advisors and officers.

The first American officer I got to know well was named Major Weiss. Major Weiss was a Special Forces officer and could speak a little bit of Arabic and we ended up being friends. One day I ended up walking into the Iraqi Operations center where General Mohan was. These Generals and higher officials were very secretive. They didn't give the Americans a lot of information. The problem was the Americans didn't know a lot about these guys and how they could not be trusted. The Americans came with clean hearts and a specific mission to accomplish. I had an idea of what these Iraqi officials were up to because I grew up with these people and I knew their history. My dad kept up on all the politics in the Iraqi Government after being in the military for so many years. He knew who these guys were and we would talk about it at home. I knew who worked for Saddam, who was in the Ba'ath Party and who was good. Many of these guys who came back to work at the MOD did not have the best interests in mind. They were there to re-gain control of the MOD.

Make no mistake there were good officers too among these guys, but something terrible started happening. These good, non-corrupted generals and high rank officials who were there to better the country all of a sudden started getting killed. They would get taken out after work on their way home from the MOD. This was the corrupt Iraqi official's game. If you were not part of their terrorist-political group they wanted you out. The corrupt people would know when you got to the MOD and when you left and they would follow you home. To officially get rid of you they would place assassins on the route the good official would take to go home and execute him or they would place a sticky bomb underneath his car. The corrupt officials would then replace the deceased officer with another official, but one from their political party. There was no place in the MOD for good people and it started to worry me a lot. What kind of future was the new Iraqi Military going to have?

My Checkpoint

The gate everyone would have to come through to enter the Ministry of Defense was called the MOD checkpoint. It was right next to Checkpoint 1 in the green zone. We pretty much shared the same Checkpoint area. I was in charge of this checkpoint and all of the security both inside and outside the building. Through the years of me over seeing my check point, many different Americans would come through and run check point 1. Everyone going into the MOD through my gate had to be checked and searched. Most of the people going through my check point were people going to work or who had business in the MOD. I would see the same faces every morning. I would have to search them and check their IDs. They would come in civilian clothes and change into military clothes inside the MOD. It was like a nine to five job. When the Generals and higher rank officials would come through my check point they didn't like getting searched by me or my men and they would complain. But this was nothing new and we dealt with it every day. The busiest time at the check points was always first thing in the morning between seven and ten. Employees, people with complaints, visitors and terrorists all showed up during those hours.

One morning we had gotten some intel that twenty children with mental disabilities were kidnapped from a local Iraqi hospital. We had been told these kids had been strapped with bombs on their bodies. These poor children had now become suicide bombers. We were also told they had been released and were wondering all over the city. This would put us in a very tough situation with these children. We looked at each other and prayed and hoped the intel information was wrong because it would have put us in a shitty position of having to protect other people.

Over the three years our check point was attacked nine times. When I say attacked I mean car bombs, suicide bombers and shootings. It was a new adventure every day. I was in charge and I would be damned if anything was getting through my check point.

The MNSTC-I found out the higher Iraqi generals and officials would give me, my men and the MP (military police), a hard time when we went to search them. So to fix this the MNSTC-I ended up bringing in a British company called Olive Security to search these guys so my men and I didn't have to do it. There would be no bias in any way when these higher officials got searched. There was only one security guy at a time from this British security company. He stood at the check point with us and was used when he was needed. At my check point we had no technology or bomb sniffing dogs. All we had was our hands, intuition and the British security company. We would use him to search the higher officers because he was not under their rank and the Iraqi generals could not give him a hard time. Over time we started to learn the different faces, their names and where they worked inside the MOD. Every day I would walk through the MOD and see Major Weiss, talk to him and patrol the entire MOD building. I would like to see what was going on and keep on top of all my favorite Iraqi officers. I say this with sarcasm, of course. One day in 2005 I ran into Major Weiss in the MOD and he explained to me his tour was ending and he would be leaving the country. He introduced me to the new major coming in named Major John Burke.

Major Burke was going to be taking a new position as military intelligence. Major Weiss was Special Forces and he worked alone and he had no other American officers with him. Major Burke had a full staff with him. He had an intelligence officer, two to three NCOs, a Sergeant Major, soldiers and other high rank officials. They were going to be moving their office from a small office inside the MOD to a larger one. They were there to watch over the Iraqi Operations center. At this time the minister of the MOD was changing too. The current Minister in the MOD was an Iraqi-British citizen named Hazim al-Shaalan and he had a British advisor. He was from the south of Iraq and lived in Britain for some time. He was a very educated and fair Minister. The MOD was safe and under control, with him in charge. He was the Minister I liked the most out of all the ministers I had served under. He was happy to have the Americans there and was happy to work with them to build a new Iraq. It was the old Iraqi Military members who were not happy to have the Americans building a new army and a new Iraq. The Iraqi government was undergoing a change in the structure of the government. The different political positions were all going to be divided evenly between the Shiites and Sunnis. So because of this change in structure the Iraqi government decided to change the Minister in the MOD. Hazim al-Shaalan was replaced by a man named Saadoun al- Dulaimi, who was from Fallujah. Al-Shaalan was a Shiite and al-Dulaimi was a Sunni. The minister's office was on the second floor of the MOD. When al-Dulaimi came in he had a huge number of security personnel with him. It was not unusual for the Minister of the MOD to have a few guys for security detail, but al-Dulaimi had a huge number of security guys. His nephew had gone and grabbed a bunch of guys from Fallujah to be his security detail. Al-Dulaimi himself didn't know a lot of them. Al-Dulaimi was not a bad guy according to his record, but his nephew brought bad guys in to the MOD to serve as his personal security. And some of those guys should not have been there. Some of these security guys were at his house inside the green zone, which made me nervous, and some were with him inside the MOD. In late 2003 and early 2004 when we fought in Fallujah, I remembered what the faces of the fighters looked like. Many of the faces in al-Dulaimi's personal security reminded me of those faces from back in Fallujah. You would look at these faces and they were not happy campers. They looked like they were up to something more.

Al-Dulaimi was a tribe in Fallujah which gave us a lot of trouble. If you remember al-Dulaimi was the officer who arrested me when I was twelve. The first American vehicle shot was by the al-Dulaimi tribe. The new Minister happened to put his nephew in charge to oversee his security detail and body guards. At the time my soldiers became concerned. We didn't know who the hell his nephew was. We knew nothing about this kid. We knew Minister al-Dulaimi was not a terrorist, but we didn't know anything about his nephew. I was lucky because there were American military personnel who stood between the MOD and the green zone. I had communicated with the Americans that I knew nothing about these guys and they looked very suspicious. I told the Americans to stop these guys and to search them well. They always seemed like they were up to something. Some of al-Dulaimi's personal security detail had green zone IDs. To get a green zone ID you had to go through a back ground check done by the American military. But many of them who were in the MOD didn't have a green zone ID and stayed in the MOD all the time. So it raised the question to us as to why these guys didn't want to have their backgrounds checked to get a green zone ID.

Working with the Americans

Major Burke was starting to get settled in the MOD. Since he was new and he knew nothing about these guys, Major Burke was there to set up the intelligence for the U.S. Army. It took him a couple of months to get the ground work completed and understand all the positions in the MOD. It was his job to figure out who worked for whom, and what other alliances they had, such as personal, family, political or religious alliances. This was a big job because the Americans didn't have a clear picture. At the time I began to talk to Major Burke more and I educated him on what was going on. I showed him around the MOD and explained things so he could get more comfortable. During this time Major Burke ended up getting promoted to Lieutenant Colonel. So now I would be helping and working with a U. S. Lt. Colonel.

At the time I remember speaking English in one of the hallways of the MOD and General Mohan over hearing me speak English. General Mohan called me over. I thought he was going to thank me for speaking to the Americans and getting everyone on the same page. Instead he asked me how I learned English. So I told him it was from studying books and speaking to the Americans here. He told me he never wanted to see me here anymore. I was shocked... I couldn't understand why he would say that to me. I was a Command sergeant major at the time. He was a higher rank than I, but I was thrown off by him saying this. Last I knew this was the new Iraqi army and we work with the Americans. It was at this moment I realized I threatened him. He didn't want me around because now he knew I would hear and understand things that he didn't want me to know. I knew from the beginning something wasn't right with him and he was up to something. But, it was clear to me now he was an enemy. I started to look at all his security detail in a much different light. They had planted themselves there and I had to watch them because I knew they would have a plan to do something in the future.

Like I said at the beginning of the book I learned how to speak English at home. My dad was an educated man. He went to a university in England in the 70s and he made us read and study English books at home and we spoke English at home also. During Saddam's time we could not speak English in the street or in public without getting into trouble. This is the reason why General Mohan lost it with me when he heard me speaking English. Speaking English for him was the equivalent of being a traitor like back in Saddam times. So I was careful about where I spoke English in the MOD around this guy. I had decided speaking English was going to be my secret around these old Ba'ath Party members. But, it was going to be one of my greatest assets when working with and helping the Americans. I was so proud and happy to have the Americans there to help us make a new Iraq for my family. I would do anything they needed to make it happen.

At the time, my commander would tell me to be careful of General Mohan and the other officers who were higher rank. He told me to always look over my shoulder. These old regime members didn't like me very much. They could put complaints against me and make trouble for me. One day in the morning I was in the Iraqi operations center with LTC Burke. One of the guys under General Mohan, named Colonel Ziyad, came in and yelled at me and LTC Burke, and asked what I was doing there. "General Mohan does not want this guy around!" So LTC Burke made me leave and stand outside. He did this out of respect for the Iraqi officers, because he couldn't understand why this high ranking Iraqi official didn't want me there. But I knew why. I told LTC Burke about what happened earlier and he said, "Why don't you come along with me and do some missions with me." I accepted his offer. It would be undercover so the Iraqis wouldn't know. He asked me if I would be willing to go out on some dangerous missions with him and help him out with translating. LTC Burke asked me because he trusted me and knew I would give him the right information. He also knew I would be able to handle the stress of some bad situations we would find ourselves in.

LTC Burke had two American interpreters, who were classified guys and there were also about a half dozen local nationals working and translating with him. But he felt the safest with me because those interpreters wouldn't be capable of a fire fight. Some of the missions we would be going on could turn bad at any second. So he and military intelligence officer LT Jason Faler had me enroll as another local national interpreter. LTC Burke felt I should get paid for the job I was doing with him since I would be going above and beyond what other interpreters were doing. I was always in my Iraqi uniform when I went on missions with LTC Burke. I only went on missions with him. Some missions required me to put on my Iraqi uniform and some the American uniform.

There was one mission I went on with LT Faler to Sadr City. It was dangerous to take LT Faler out because he spoke fluent Egyptian Arabic. So if we took him out it would be a dead giveaway he was either intelligence or CIA. Having a guy with blue eyes and blonde hair speaking fluent Arabic was like walking around with a bulls-eye on your ass. He would have been a prime target. We couldn't let him go out on too many missions because it was taking a big chance.

On the missions I went on with LTC Burke we would end up going to all different bases all over the country. We went to Mosul to get a terrorist who was killing people. We handled the election militias all over Iraq and we did all kinds of investigations. We had a good working relationship and we got a lot of work accomplished. In the early half of 2005 it was a different environment at the MOD than what I expected. In the back of my head I always thought about what General Mohan said to me. It always bothered me and ate at me. I was always thinking of what he could be up to. So my MP guys and I always kept a close eye on him.

It was right around this time LTC Burke had invited me to go out on a four day mission with him. This mission would entail having to negotiate with terrorists. I was not only a translator for LTC Burke but I also became personal security for him too. I had lived with these faces for so long I began to learn what the dangerous faces looked like. I studied them like I use to study those wolves. I could read them, I would listen to them and from this I could begin to understand what they were thinking and what their agenda was. They became predictable in a way. I knew how they worked and every day I got more of an education from them at the MOD. I started to identify what political parties they belonged to. What alliances they had in the MOD and outside. Many of these guys did belong to some big terrorist organizations. They were not to be screwed around with. If they wanted you dead they would make it happen.

8

Four Day Mission

We were in the office one day and we got a call from an American Lieutenant Colonel, who was the commander of the 1- 103rd Armor battalion in Baiji, north of Tikrit, Iraq. He and his command had been ambushed by some insurgents. Baiji, Iraq happens to be the site of a very large oil refining facility and it also happens to be the site where the oil pipe lines from Kirkuk meet and go south to Baghdad for more refining and use, and north to Turkey for export sales.

This LTC in Baiji and his guys took some papers off the guys they had captured during the ambush. It turned out these guys were being paid by the Ministry of Defense. LTC Burke found this interesting because he didn't have troops in this area getting paid, so something was not right. LTC Burke went to the MOD personnel office to find out what was going on. Sure enough they were on the payroll. He started doing research with the personnel office and MOD and found out there was a 3 star Iraqi General (LTG Daham) who worked as the special advisor to the MOD before al-Dulaimi became the Minister.

He found out, speaking to the prior minister al-Shaalan, there was a whole new part of the Iraqi army created which no one knew about. LTC Burke had eight authorized divisions of the Iraqi army spread throughout the country and two more divisions were being created based upon what the thoughts of the American need was. As LTC Burke was doing his investigation into this new division of the Iraqi army, a private company was brought in to Iraq and they were contracted to rebuild the entire Iraqi oil infrastructure and refurbish the pipe line. So what LTC Burke had found out from these contractors was that the Iraqi army had built ten battalions. These battalions made up a division which provided security for these oil pipe lines. It was a very interesting find because no one knew about them. The Iraqis were siphoning their funding to pay them from the operations money that was being kept in the basement of the MOD. This money which America had provided to the MOD was not being very well tracked.

What had happened in the ambush earlier was one of these Iraqi Battalions who were hired to protect the pipe line had shot up one of the American battalions in Baiji. The oil pipe lines were not the only thing coming under attack at this time. The power lines had been under attack also. The oil lines and the power lines ran parallel to each other. There was about one million barrels of oil moving a day through the pipe lines which came from the port of Basra, in the south of Iraq.

LTC Burke got approval to put together a mission because he had identified all 10 battalions, where their headquarters were and the infrastructure that supported them. So it was LTC Burke's mission to find out who these oil battalions were, who supported them and who they knew. So we had to coordinate with the 3rd infantry division who controlled everything up to Taji and the 42nd infantry division, a National Guard division out of Albany, New York. The road trip for this mission was arranged with General Ayad, the Iraqi army's operations officer (the G3) and LTC. LTC Burke and I ended up working for him on this mission. So our road trip team consisted of General Ayad, some other Iraqi generals and some shady Iraqi Colonel who was attached to the pipeline security. Our goal for this mission was to go and check all these ten battalions from Kirkuk all the way down to Baghdad.

The Road Trip

On April 27, 2005 we went to Baiji first, because Baiji was the hub. As we were out starting our mission we get a report saying the pipeline had been bombed, "It's all on fire!"

So, as we got up to the pipeline in Baiji, we discovered the real truth. The truth was an Iraqi oil private, in one of these battalions was smoking a cigarette near the pipeline. He flicked his butt away after smoking, not realizing there is natural gas around the pipe line. So, the natural gas explodes, blowing up the pipe line. There was no terrorist attack it was a weak battalion infrastructure with untrained soldiers guarding it. There was another incident to investigate also where the electrical power went down. What happened there was someone wrapped a couple of packs of Semtex with duct tape and a detonator wired to explode. They figured out if you take out one leg of an electrical tower, the tower topples over, cutting off the electric. This was done by one of the oil security battalions because they felt they were not getting paid enough. They had made up a story saying they got attacked in order to negotiate a higher price to contract more security for it from the oil company in Iraq.

The Iraqi oil company north was owned by the Sunni part of the government and the Iraqi oil company south was owned by the Shiite part of the government which ran from the southern part of Baghdad all the way down to Basra. What was interesting is the Shiite portion never sustained an attack. The northern oil company territory operated by the Sunnis was attacked every day. It became apparent the people in these battalions protecting the pipe lines were locals and some were good people and some were not. So the guys guarding the pipeline, if they felt they weren't paid enough, would attack the pipeline and create problems. It was very clear this was a money game. The U.S. was paying for ten thousand people to protect these pipelines, which would be one thousand people per battalion. However, in reality all there was protecting the pipelines were two guards with rifles. No night vision gear, no communications and maybe a machine gun on occasion. So it made us question who was getting paid for ten thousand people.

Kirkuk

We get to Kirkuk and we were fortunate enough not to get attacked on our way up there. We taught the guys up there reactive contact drills, so if there was an attack everyone protecting the pipeline would know how to respond. The response we would get from us being there would vary from base to base. One base near Baiji wouldn't let any Iraqi eat in their dining hall. The Iraqi generals and I would have to eat outside the dining hall. At a different base all the men would get up and salute the Iraqi Generals. Each base was different, and each battalion under each base was different. Because we were so out in the wilderness at some of these bases and battalions, we were way over our time line and at one point one of the battalion commanders wanted to leave LTC Burke and I at a site and head back to Baiji. So LTC

Burke had to threaten to call the Corps Commander and have him fired.

We finished our work and headed back to Baiji. This brought us to the end of day three. So, the beginning of day four we start heading back down Route Tampa from Baiji toward Baghdad. We made it to our 8th battalion to visit and this battalion was very far off the pipeline. This was abnormal because the bases should sit right on or very near the pipeline. The outfits these guys were wearing weren't Iraqi army uniforms. The whole thing didn't feel right at all. We go in and have our meeting. We had a combat camera with us and LTC Burke instructed our guys to watch everyone's movements. He also told everyone be ready to fight in case this meeting goes sour. There was this aura around the whole compound which made you feel something was not right here.

Route Tampa

After we left the compound and got back on to route Tampa we were attacked by a suicide car bomber, otherwise known as a vehicle born improvised explosive device (VBIED) and right after that an ambush of insurgents. Our convoy was made up of three SUV trucks and four (High Mobility Multipurpose Wheeled Vehicle) HMMWVs. There was a HMMWV in front of us, then our SUV, a HMMWV behind us, and it alternated like that. So all of a sudden we see a car come screaming at us. The driver of our SUV, Tyrone Knipping, was from New Jersey and he was a young guy with great driving skills. Tyrone all of a sudden sees a red car coming at us on our right. Tyrone speeds up and swerves taking us down an embankment and up the other side to the opposite side of Route Tampa. The car bomb swerves, because if he goes down the embankment, any jiggle to the car will set the bomb off and he wouldn't have hit anyone. So the car bomb swerved going straight into the HMMWV which was behind us.

I saw the trailing HMMWV explode into flames. I saw the car bomb driver go flying into the air too. So Knipping turns our SUV around and we go back. No sooner than we get back to the site and get out of the vehicle, a fire fight ensues on us. This is all being caught on the combat camera, every second of it. The American base near us saw what was going on and sent out tanks and Apaches to us from Taji. The Lieutenant who was in the HMMWV behind us was stuck in the passenger seat and his foot and leg were injured. The gunner had burns on his face and head and I am not sure if he survived or not. The driver of the HMMWV had blood pouring from his neck from shrapnel hitting him. The HMMWV door next to the Lieutenant was melted shut and we had to pry it open with a crow bar. While we were trying to triage these guys and waiting for the medivac to come, the shitty fire fight continued. A few minutes later we had tanks and an Apache come in and the fire fight was over. Later after the last battalion visits we figured out this little guy who was a colonel in the Iraqi army and our guide on this mission was in charge of the whole battalion and the whole area of the oil security network. The biggest kicker was he was the one who set up the whole entire ambush on us. He targeted our SUV because he wanted to get General Ayad. Every corrupt person in the Iraqi military wanted General Ayad dead and for no good reason except he was a good guy, working for the good of Iraq and doing his job. General Mohan was successful in assassinating General Ayad after our four day mission. After General Ayad's assassination LTC Burke had General Mohan red listed. Mohan now was unable to do anything in the MOD.

LTC Burke always included me in a lot of the different trainings he was doing and had me work a lot with him. He felt at one point after this four day mission I needed a few days off. I was working pretty hard. I was holding down security at the MOD and going out on missions with LTC Burke. I didn't have any downtime except to sleep for a few hours each night. A conference was coming up in Germany. A few of the Iraqi Generals and Zebari, the Army Chief of Staff would be going to this conference to meet with General George W. Casey Jr. and other American officers. LTC

Burke felt it would be a great opportunity for me to go and be a translator for these Generals. I was someone they could trust and I would get a fair amount of education out of this also. At this conference different topics would be discussed. The big topic the Generals would be speaking about was how to decrease the number of casualties, both American and Iraqi. So I took a few days off and I went. It was great. Germany was beautiful and it was some much needed time away. I got to speak to General Casey also. General Casey had asked the Iraqi generals what they needed the most to protect their soldiers in battle and why. I couldn't have jumped any quicker to answer the question. The Iraqi generals fumbled around the answer. I was the only one at the table who had been on the front lines and knew what we needed and why. None of the Generals had been to the battle. They had heard and spoken about it, but they had never been in the middle of it to understand what we needed. I told him we were in desperate need of armored vehicles. At the time we used Nissan pick-up trucks. The pick-up trucks didn't offer any protection if we were getting shot at. I explained to him a pick-up truck would hold eight guys in it. Two in the front and six in the back. If we were driving there was no protection for the guys in the back getting shot at, and if we were hit by an RPG all eight of us would be dead. So I explained to him if it we were attacked in an armored vehicle the gunner might be the only one killed but seven other lives would be saved. General Casey thought it was a reasonable explanation as to why we needed them and a month later we had armored vehicles.

I also had a chance to speak to other officers in the American military. Since I was the only NCO at this conference who had been on the front lines I had a lot of officers asking me questions. I met with Brigade Commanders and Battalion Commanders. They had soldiers who were in training and were getting deployed to Iraq in the near future. They asked me questions about the cities they were getting deployed to. I was able to give them all kinds of valuable information which they needed to know. I was able to tell them what tribes were there, which tribes would cooperate with them, what the weather and conditions were like and what challenges they would be up against. After Germany they took this information back to the role players at their base and created scenarios based off my information for real life simulation. They wanted their soldiers to be prepared and understand what they were going to be facing. Talking to these guys was another invaluable experience for me. They had such concern for their soldiers. These commanders wanted to make sure their soldiers could get the job done, be safe doing it and make it home to their families. I was so impressed with how they cared about their guys. I thought to myself my higher officers could give a good shit if I lived or died.

One evening, while the Iraqi Generals were eating dinner and drinking, I sat outside of the hotel enjoying the peace and quiet. It had been such a long time since I hadn't heard explosions, yelling and loud vehicles. A few minutes later a car of American soldiers pulled up and asked me if I wanted to go out in Wiesbaden. I figured why not and they told me to meet them at the end of the street in a few minutes. They took me out to a night club. I had never been to a night club before. Everyone was dancing, partying and having a good time. I stood there and stared. I couldn't believe how cool it was. I felt so bad for my soldiers because they were back home fighting for their lives and here in Germany there was no care in the world. Everyone was dancing and having fun. I had a German girl come ask me to dance and I didn't even know how to dance. Germany was a terrific experience and I have great memories forever.

After I got back from Germany, the generals I had gone with told the other generals I was there. This created a big headache for me. Those corrupt generals thought I had received training to become a spy for the U.S. Intelligence. Little did they know I was already ten steps ahead of them! Zebari was there and he knew what was going on and what went on at the conference. I had no worries, but those generals were on me. They gave me such a hard time and kept treating me as an enemy. It was fine with me I wanted to get rid of them too. The feeling was mutual between us.

I Smell the Enemy

The dozen or so guys who trained with me, and who were my current PSD team, were working as security detail for the high ranking Iraqi officials. They were acting as security inside the MOD and they were always watching all of these guys and their every move also. My communication with my PSD team was always on. We were men who trained together and fought together. We had a very good network inside the MOD. My PSD team knew we were surrounded by all kinds of terrorist groups and we couldn't keep up. We worked together watching them and informing each other. There were a lot of misunderstandings with the security detail for General Mohan and other officials and these people looked at me and my PSD team with hate.

The Major

There were a lot of obstacles in the Iraqi government at the time due to the resistance the corrupt officers had to Americans being there. We knew things wouldn't be smooth, but these guys spoke and acted like our old Ba'ath party friends. There was one guy in charge of security for the Minister of Defense. He was one of Minister al-Dulaimi's extended family and his name was Major Sabbah. Both of these men were from Fallujah and Ramadi, Iraq. Major Sabbah always raised his voice and was always unhappy being around the Americans. The look on his face always looked like he couldn't believe where he was standing. At the time the MOD started getting attacked by mortars. In order for mortars to fly people have to give coordinates. The mortars would tend to fly the most when people were going out to lunch, leaving the MOD and walking to the green zone. What was interesting was neither Major Sabbah nor his men would be outside at lunch when these mortars were dropping. It was a give-away they had some hand in this even though they would pretend they didn't. It was pretty hard to keep track of all the different terrorists in the MOD. We had to make a priority list of who we had to keep our eyes on. Because you didn't know who was up to what.

The pressure I was under by being in charge of security for both inside and outside the MOD was tremendous. There were so many unprotected Americans working in the MOD in departments which had many Iraqis and very few Americans. The corrupt Iraqis and terrorists who planted themselves in this building were like the wolves and they were looking at these unarmed Americans like the sheep. My PSD team and I had to keep constant tabs on everyone we thought was a threat. But sometimes it was impossible to watch them all. Major Sabbah had his own groups of terrorists in the MOD and we were pretty sure Major Sabbah was not going to be there long. He was there to get a touchdown, meaning he was there for the big score and once he got his touchdown he was out! But what was he looking to do?

I had to speak to my PSD team to start watching the activity of Major Sabbah and his people. I almost lost one of my PSD guys to one of the mortars. Many of these mortars injured my soldiers and some of them had to be taken to the hospital. You would walk outside, someone would give them the coordinates of where you were standing and the mortar would land on you. Major Sabbah began to look and act very suspicious. All of a sudden one day he started looking for sensitive locations inside the MOD for his security detail. All the locations he requested to move his security detail to were next to t-walls and the river. We had plenty of space inside the MOD so what was he up to? Why did he need these rooms in the MOD? My guys and I knew for a fact we had terrorists planted in the MOD and we had to scrutinize every move and everything they said. They were not known terrorists but they had very big ties to the wrong political parties outside of the MOD and those ties were big terrorist organizations. There was one time Major Sabbah was adamant about getting this one room where my guys slept who worked the watch tower. It was next to a t-wall and it was the only room that would take us to the watch tower. I had to do something to prevent Major Sabbah from getting any of these locations. I would challenge the higher authority in the MOD stating I needed these locations for my men and the job they were doing. After I went to the higher authority Major Sabbah gave us a break on wanting these locations, but we knew there would be something else up his sleeve.

I always warned LTC Burke he had a lot of bad people around him and to be careful. I spoke to him about this one colonel who was working around his staff quite often named Col. Ziyad. Ziyad was someone who was very suspicious. We had a lot of work watching over Major Sabbah, General Mohan and Colonel Ziyad. Even though General Mohan was red listed at this time, he still had people in the building working for him.

General Martin E. Dempsey, Chairman of the Joint Chiefs of Staff and I back in 2006, as he presents me with a certificate from the Anti-terrorism First Protection course.

Right to left: General Daniel Bolger, General Mubder al Dulaimi and I. (2006)

LTC John Burke and I in Ramadi. (2005)

General Casey, Zebari and I at the conference in Germany. (2005)

LT Jason Faler and I in Sadr City, Baghdad, Iraq.

Tyrone Knipping and I in Tikrit on the Four day Mission. (2005)

Major Megan McClung, Jeremy Reyes (right) and I (2004)

Gunnery Instructor Kevin Smalling, A PSD member Frkan al Kraawi and I.

Me sitting in Saddam's chair at Camp Victory. This was previously Al Faw Palace. This was one of the palaces where Saddam would stay.

My PSD team after we completed training with our instructor Gunnery Sergeant Kevin Smalling in the center.

LTC Burke and I at Saddam's palace in his home town of Tikrit. (2005)

My friend "The Rock" Khalid (right) and I (left).

Me visiting Megan's grave site for the first time in 2010.

Me with an American looking through the scope at possible threats near our check points.

9

Saving the American Officer

Major Sabbah had orders to stay in the Iraqi Minister of Defense office in the MOD but instead we always saw him walking all over the MOD. Always looking and investigating. He looked like a rat snooping around and sniffing. At the time we felt like he was looking for ways out of the MOD. He was always walking around the borders of the MOD and always looking at the red zone areas. If you were to leave the MOD to go to the green zone you would be stopped and searched by American officers. If you were to leave the MOD and go to the red zone you could be stopped and searched by my officers. Sabbah seemed like he was always trying to avoid this. Cars and vehicles could not enter the MOD unless they came in through the green zone and were checked by the Americans first. It was pretty difficult for someone to get something inside the MOD. It wasn't impossible to get something in or out, but we tried to make it as difficult as possible. It seemed like Sabbah was trying to get something out of the MOD without being noticed, stopped or searched, but we couldn't figure out what. My guys and I watched their every move. They were now on our radar. Sabbah's moves were so suspicious.

T-Wall Truck

One day out of the blue, in the evening, we saw a vehicle. It was a large truck which came in from the green zone gate. It was a specific truck that moved t-walls and heavy items. T-walls were like tall concrete barriers. This truck was ordered in by the Minister of Defense's office, and Sabbah had this vehicle park at a specific location next to the MOD. When I saw Sabbah talking to the driver it made me feel like something involving Americans was going to go down soon. The truck happened to be parked at a location Sabbah wanted a few weeks before and I wouldn't give it to him. I was in charge of security for the whole perimeter of the MOD. Why wasn't I told about this vehicle coming into the MOD and why didn't anyone tell me we needed it? Sabbah ordered the truck driver to stay in the vehicle at all times. Because I had no official word as to why the truck had been brought in I told my PSD team to shoot the truck driver if he started to move the truck towards the t-wall. I felt the truck was brought in to carry out a plan. If this was official business I would have heard about it. A few minutes later an

134

armored Mercedes from the MOD shows up and parks next to the t-wall truck. At the time Sabbah's guys told my guards they were going to be removing and carrying out some furniture from inside the MOD. This made no sense at the time. Let's recap this! Moving furniture at night out of the MOD, needing a truck which moves t-walls to do it and I had no official notification at all! It looked to me like the stars were aligning to light up my night! Located next to where the truck was and behind the t-wall and watch tower was an abandoned road which lead straight out to the red zone. I kept trying to call LTC Burke but he was not answering his phone.

After seeing all this unfold we kept watching Sabbah and his guys. They were walking fast all over the MOD and they looked nervous. They didn't look normal to us. Sabbah had some of his security guys switching shifts that day. This meant his guys would come for two weeks, work security and go home for two weeks. Since it was a security shift day, the security guys would help Sabbah carry out his plan and then disappear for a couple of weeks. There would be no one around to question and no one would know what had happened. Sabbah had a truck which lifted t-walls, he also had the armored Mercedes which belonged to the MOD parked next to the t-wall and there was a high level of tension in the building..... A plan was about to take action and we had to figure it out quick.

Ready to Engage

My guys and I geared up with our guns, Kevlar and all necessary gear. It was around 10:45 at night and there were too many of Sabbah's guys in the MOD. We got ready to enter a fire fight. I knew two of LTC Burke's staff were in his office. I thought maybe they were looking to do something to LTC Burke's staff. I had gotten to know all these guys pretty well and I wasn't going to let anything happen to one of them. So I sent five of my PSD team to scan the MOD. I needed to know if there were any other Americans in the building. I told my guys if you don't find any other Americans in the building go back to Burke's office. I sent two guys upstairs and three guys downstairs. A few minutes later over the radio one of my guys who went upstairs told me there was a light on. It was an American Colonel working on the second floor and he was alone.

My PSD guy over our radios stated, "Shit, they took the lock off and unlocked the door up here!" He had noticed a door which should be locked at all times was open. This door, which was unlocked, went to a stairway that brought you down the back of the MOD to the t-walls. The plot was starting to reveal itself.

I replied, "Ok we are on the way!" And we started to head up to the second floor.

My PSD guy said, "Gear up, I think this is going to be a heavy gun fight!"

The Abduction Plan

So right away the picture was clear to us and we figured out their plan. It was not Burke's guys Sabbah and his guys wanted to get. It was the full bird colonel on the second floor who worked late and alone. Sabbah and his guys were going to go for a high ranking American colonel. Capturing a high level official held more weight for them when it came time to trade him for al Qaeda members the U.S. had captured or when asking for a high ransom amount. Who knew how long they would hold him for? If they were successful it would have been the greatest kidnapping of all time for them. It would have been the touchdown Sabbah was looking for. It would have been a disaster for the U.S. The colonel, at his location in the MOD, was quite a distance from the green zone. These U.S. officers and advisors had an office in the MOD and also in the MNSTC-I. I had not worked with this Colonel before. I had only seen him a couple of times but he was always nice and respectful to me. I figured he must have a wife and family back home in America and we had to get him the hell out of there. Sabbah's plan was to go up the back stairwell, grab the officer, bring him back down the stair well to the back of the building, put the officer in the armored Mercedes, have the truck lift the t-wall so the Mercedes could exit the MOD under the lifted t-wall and proceed on to the road which went straight into the red zone.

The Americans would have never figured out what happened or how the American officer was taken. Sabbah and his guys would have never been searched between Baghdad and Ramadi because they carried the Minister of Defense Office ID. The Iraqi check points would have opened the way for them and the officer would never be found. Why would they want to do this? For retaliation for a family member who was killed in Fallujah? Or for trading a big al Qaeda member? Either way I didn't want to find out the answers to those questions.

Get the American Out Now

So, the rest of my guys and I ran up to the second floor. My guys and I were trying to figure out as we were running up there how we were going to approach this Colonel without freaking him out. As we were approaching the colonel's door, one of my guys looked at me and said, "Sergeant major you do realize after this we are going to be going to war with one of the biggest terrorist organizations in the world?"

It was at this moment we were all very nervous because we were fucking with a giant. We figured we were all dead. If a fire fight started with Sabbah's team, there were 50 of them and only a dozen of us. I entered the Colonel's office and I said, "Excuse me sir, it's very late, we are getting ready to close up for the night and I need to take you out of here now! Right now!"

The Colonel looked at me said, "Absolutely!" He grabbed his laptop and bag and we were gone. As we were walking the colonel asked me, "Is everything is alright?"

Trying to keep as calm as I could I said, "It will be once I get you out of here. We have a possible security threat in the building. If anything should happen keep walking to the American soldiers and don't stop until you get to them."

I took him out through the front entrance of the MOD to the green zone knowing Sabbah's guys were coming up the back stairwell. Two of my guys stayed behind at the colonel's door so if they ran after us they would have to go through my two guys first. No sooner than we left some of Sabbah's guys came up the back stairwell and through the unlocked door. They were shocked to see my two guys, all geared up staring back at them. Sabbah's guys pulled back and turned around to go back down the stairwell and back to where Sabbah was.

Sabbah was smart enough to stand down and not start a fire fight. The Americans would hear and see the fire fight going on in the MOD and the American QRF team would engage in seconds. This would also expose Sabbah and his men for who they were. We got the U.S. Colonel back to the green zone and he was safe. As my guys and I walked back from the green zone Sabbah and his guys watched us and looked right at us. He now knew who we were and he knew our faces. My PSD guys were so scared and they looked at me and said, "We are dead and we realize we did this for you. We didn't know this guy, and we didn't have to do this, but we supported you."

Believe me when I say I know my guys put their lives on the line for me. I didn't want to see anything happen to any of them. They all had families to go home to. We all knew at some point in the future al-Qaeda would get us, but this put us on the fast track to death.

I'm a Dead Man

After all the excitement with the Colonel my PSD guys and I went back to the barracks inside the MOD. The U.S. colonel was not supposed to be in the MOD late at night. Only LTC Burke's guys stayed for the overnight shift. He needed to be in the MNSTC-I at the time. I never told anyone who the officer was because the officer could have gotten in some serious trouble. If the Colonel was taken by Sabbah and his men, it would have been an absolute disaster for the U.S. military, as well as a huge media frenzy, and who knows what they would have done to him.

I kept trying to call LTC Burke all night long on his DSN line, but I never got in touch with him. I needed to notify him of what happened before something happened to me. Sabbah could have come back and killed me and my PSD guys at some point through the night. We figured Sabbah had to be pissed because we foiled his plan. Early the next morning LTC Burke called me and I met with him the first moment I could. I told him what events had gone down the night before and I also told him about Col. Sabbah's plan to abduct an American within the next 24 hours. I told him straight up, "al-Dulaimi wants one of you guys." I was giving him this information and he needed to do what he needed to do with it. I explained to him this was critical. Something was going to happen in the upcoming 24 hours and at night. I told him the enemy is all around him and his men every day and something needs to be done. Burke had realized his life and all the Americans in the MOD were in danger.

At first Burke listened to me and after speaking to me he was able to verify the information I gave him. I gave him facts which Burke knew nobody else would have known about. It verified my story on the spot. He had my information verified in about thirty to forty minutes. So Burke got on the phone with his boss and a few minutes later they were on the phone with current U.S. commanding general's office. Within forty minutes after speaking to the commanding general's office Burke's office had the whole MOD emptied of all American workers.

LTC Burke and his team had to stay in the MOD to continue the investigation but they were suited up in full gear. I always gave Burke the best intelligence information, but because I was not an A1 source and I was foreign he would have to verify it first. Sometimes the verification process would take time, but my verification came back spot on at that moment.

The information I had given LTC Burke was handed off to Lieutenant Faler. LT Faler got on the phone with a guy he had worked with before at the OGA (Other Government Agencies). From there he was directed to contact people at the DIA (Defense Intelligence Agency). After speaking to the DIA he was directed to speak to the Counter Intelligence Military Personnel. A meeting was set up between LT Faler and the intelligence officers. LT Faler wanted to meet with the intelligence officers first before he introduced them to me. He wanted to make sure I would be safe and not exposed to any danger or compromised in any way for giving them information. Later LT Faler explained to me intelligence guys do not befriend anyone they are working with, but I was different. He trusted me, we became friends, and because of the loyalty factor this changed the game a bit because he didn't want to see me put in harm's way for helping with higher intelligence.

Once LT Faler felt good after meeting with them he got in touch with me. He told me some higher intelligence officers would be contacting me and they needed all the information I had. I was anxious to speak with them because I wanted to make sure no one else would be abducted from the MOD.

Here is a quote from MAJ Faler in regards to us working together and the intelligence information:

In 2005, while deployed as an Intelligence Officer with the 53rd Army Liaison Team attached to the XVIII Airborne Corps, embedded in the Joint Headquarters in the Iraqi Ministry of Defense as part of Operation Iraqi Freedom, I had the very good fortune and privilege of befriending Hamody. At the time, Hamody was a Sergeant Major and a warrior with a reputation and significant combat credibility. He spoke excellent English, and I spoke near-fluent Egyptian Arabic. He quickly became a reliable friend--much like a brother--and also source of information that was hard to come by for people like myself in the threat environment at the time. A time came when

143

Hamody relayed to me that he had some information that was of high value and importance, and was time-sensitive. Because of my role and the location where I was embedded, I had developed a number of relationships with people in many organizations within the coalition, both military and civilian, to include individuals and teams throughout the intelligence community. I contacted two individuals from a civilian US intelligence organization with whom I had previously worked on another issue. I informed them of some generalities concerning the information that Hamody relayed to me and they were immediately interested in speaking with him. Because the information had a nexus with individuals in Anbar Province, where the US Marine Corps were heavily engaged in the fight, they told me that they wanted to bring two other individuals from the intelligence community who were currently highly involved in anything intelligence-related having an Anbar Province nexus. These two individuals--a male and a female--made arrangements to travel from Anbar Province to the IZ (International Zone) to meet with Hamody. A short time later, I picked them up from an LZ (Landing Zone) in the International Zone, drove them to a compound within the IZ, and briefed them on my relationship with Hamody, and generalities concerning the information Hamody claimed to hold. I suppose that I was interviewing them as much as they were interviewing me at the time. Hamody had become a very close friend and was in constant jeopardy, and I was not about to hand him off to amateurs or anyone who took his safety lightly. The two individuals, who were uniformed members of the uniformed US military (as opposed to civilian intelligence operators), seemed trustworthy as far as I could tell from this meeting and I put Hamody in touch with them. After they made contact with Hamody, I neither asked them nor Hamody what was said or about any other details. This is common practice in the intelligence community. I did, however, at some point thereafter, receive an e-mail from one of the individuals involved, via a secure channel, and the message essentially thanked me for connecting them with Hamody, and that the information he had provided was truly excellent.

Although I had almost daily contact with Hamody after that, I didn't converse with him about this topic, but it is my understanding that he subsequently met many times with these individuals and possibly others in the US intelligence community.

MAJ Jason Faler

Here is a Quote from LTC Joh Burke in regards to the officer almost being kidnapped:

I first met SGM Hamody Jasim in January 2005. At the time I was the Senior Liaison officer (Executive Officer) for the 53rd Army Liaison Team (53rd ALT), assigned in Direct Support of XVIII Airborne Corps Headquarters, Baghdad, Iraq. The 53rd ALT maintained three Liaison teams within each of the Iraqi Ministry of the Interior (MOI), Ministry of Defense (MOD) and the Prime Ministers Situation Room (PMSR). We had numerous assigned missions. We maintained situational awareness of Iraqi Military, Police and Political operations in Iraq at the highest levels of Government. We advised and trained our General and Field Grade Officer Counterparts. We step up and maintained intelligence gathering operations in support of Multinational Corps Iraq (MNCI) and Multinational Force Iraq (MNFI). We also coordinated daily with LTG Petraeus' Command, the Multinational Security Training Command-Iraq (MNSTC-I) at Camp Phoenix. These operations were designed to support and assist both MNCI's and MNFI's Campaign Plans for Iraq.

It was my honor to lead the Liaison Team assigned to the Iraqi Ministry of Defense. In my position I attended and briefed the General Babaker Zebari, the Iraqi Chairman of their Joint Chiefs of Staff and both Iraqi Ministers of Defense during my tour. I also attended and briefed at all major Iraqi

General Staff meetings. I briefed and coordinated with the most
Senior Iraqi General Officers on a daily basis. I also was a
regular attendee, representing the Ministry of Defense (MOD)
at the Iraqi Governmental Deputies Meetings every Tuesday
when I was in Baghdad. Two early missions we conducted were
to develop an awareness of who actually worked at the MOD
and more importantly who at the Political and Governmental
level they actually worked for and reported to; and visit, assess
and report on the multiple political militia units formed by the
Politicians seeking election for office in January 2005. The goal
in this assignment was to render an assessment whether the
militia could be assimilated into the MNSTC-I/MNCI plans for
the Iraqi Armed forces, or forced to disband.

At this time, SGM Hamody worked as the Military
Police (MP) Company SGM that provided interior and exterior
security for the Ministry of Defense. SGM Hamody was one of
the first enlisted by the U.S. Marines into the New Iraqi Army.
As one of the original members of the New Iraqi Army, and
speaking fluent English, Hamody was quickly promoted to the
Rank of SGM. He was 17 to 18 years old at the time. In the U.S.
Army, a SGM is normally in their 15-20th year of service and
between 31-40 years old. This was a staggering disparity.
Nonetheless SGM Hamody had trained, supplied and led his
MP Company since inception.

I was introduced to SGM Hamody by the Special
Forces Major I was replacing after he had successfully

completed his tour of duty. SGM Hamody became a key advisor to my team within the Ministry based upon his ability to speak freely with us in English and his knowledge of the real inner working of the MOD. My Intelligence Officer, Second Lieutenant (2LT) Jason Faler, a fluent Arabic Speaker, quickly confirmed the veracity of Hamody's information. (For months we hid knowledge of his Arabic fluency as a double check upon the numerous interpreters and Iraqi officers we managed at the MOD.) SGM Hamody also quickly volunteered to accompany me on my numerous trips into Iraq as I visited, assessed and reported on all the political militia units and the more formal Iraqi Army brigades. His combat acumen, fluency and comradeship contributed incomparably to the ultimate success of my team.

It was considered a normal duty that Hamody accompanied me whenever I left the green Zone. We were virtually inseparable. As such I had the opportunity to introduce him to the Coalition and American Officers I frequently interacted with to the General Officer and Field Grade level at MNCI, MNFI and MNSTC-I. Everyone he met was quickly impressed with his knowledge, trustworthiness and patriotism. While this grew his reputation with the Coalition, it also became resented by many Iraqi Generals within the MOD.

This animosity was a factor of Iraqi army tradition, politics and his age. He had clearly exceeded traditional Iraqi boundaries and was acting more as an American Non-

Commissioned Offer than an Iraqi. This caused more than one Iraqi general to express their discontent with him to me. I quickly assured them that he worked for me, and I worked for the Iraqi Chief of Staff, General Babaker. That was normally enough to reinforce my position. The two key Iraqi generals were Babaker and Nasir Abadi. On about 24 September 2005, I was advised by Hamody that elements within the MOD and the Minister of Defenses Personal Security Detachment were both monitoring the movements of and planning the actual kidnapping of one of the US Army colonels assigned to the MOD by MNSTC-I. At the time there were at least 40 to 50 Coalition military advisors assigned by MNSTC-I to train and mentor the Iraqi General Staff. When I first received this report, I admit I was skeptical. While I trusted SGM Hamody with my life, he was also a very young man and knew of the animus much of the MOD staff held for him. It took my team about 15 minutes to confirm enough of his information that I quickly contacted my superior officer, Colonel Peter, and my counterparts at MNSTCI of this new Intelligence. Their response was immediate. They ordered all Coalition advisors out of the MOD for two days, except my team for monitoring purposes, and limited travel within the Green Zone to more the two personnel (They banned single personnel travel). After this, operations within the MOD returned to normal.

This was a significant event. It was a constant concern that as military advisors trained and mentored the Iraqis, often living and eating and sleeping with them, that we could be compromised. Both MNCI and MNFI had contingency plans regarding the recovery of personnel, Whereabouts Unknown (DUSTWUN). These plans basically would stop all non-critical operational and focus all military power to recover our lost personnel. The fact that this person was an Army colonel would have caused havoc within the Combat Advisor Community. Trust is the glue that held these operations together. Imagine your feelings after such an event, walking into an Iraqi building or camp with just your pistol, daily, to do your job. With no external support beyond your personal experience, training and wit.

I know after my team came home in January 2006, that SGM Hamody remained as a trusted advisor to our replacements, and more importantly, to MNSTC-I. He maintained his relationships with the officers I introduced him to, and he continued to provide valuable intelligence and insight through the next few years. This led him into a position of trust within the Coalition, and of danger within his own Army. The MOD as a whole quickly considered him more of an American asset, than an Iraqi one. Such that Hamody ended up transferring and moving to live on an American FOB and specifically only supporting American teams.

At the end, I consider SGM Hamody somewhere between a surrogate son and best friend. He is about 18 months older than my eldest son, yet our shared experiences in combat solidified a relationship that endures today. Jason Faler and I were instrumental to gaining him an "Interpreters Visa" that allowed SGM Hamody to enter the United States, where he now maintains permanent residence and supports his new family. I am certain today that without SGM Hamody my tour in Iraq would have been quite a different experience. Potentially fatally so. Iraq in 2005 was on the brink of the Civil War that tore it apart after the bombing of the Golden Mosque in 2006.

John H. Burke COL U.S Army (Retired)

10

Unknown U.S. Intelligence Officers

I was contacted by phone soon after talking to LT Faler. About an hour after that a car all blacked out, with two intelligence agents (a male and female), picked me up and took me to an unknown location within the green zone. The car they picked me up in had a screen on the dash board which scanned, at a distance, all objects in front of and around the car. It scanned the objects for explosives. I had never seen anything before like this in my life. These agents showed up in civilian clothes, but I figured they had to be someone big because the military didn't even have this kind of technology. At a certain point while we were driving they put up a screen between me and them so I couldn't see where they were taking me. It was a villa within a compound the officers took me to. Prior to the war it was special guard housing during Saddam times. There was a third agent at the villa when we got there. The place they took me to was well secured and looked like it was only used for official business.

It was a high security clearance area only for classified people and information. They had me sit in a room and by the look on their faces I could see they had an idea of what was going on. I had no idea who the agents were, where they came from or what department they were from. I had never seen these faces in the green zone before. I told them everything I knew and they were hungry and excited for any information I could give them. Right away we started identifying the officers in the MOD who were part of the terrorist organizations. I had to give them the full family names of these people and where they were from.

Can you work for us?

We started with Sabbah. The intelligence officers needed to know who Sabbah worked for back in Saddam's time and what connections he had. When I told her I knew Sabbah was from Fallujah, she stopped writing, looked straight at me and said "From Fallujah?"

I looked at her straight in the eye and said, "Yes, Why?" I had no idea these agents were operating in the Fallujah/Ramadi area. In that area the al-Dulaimi tribes were leading the biggest battle against the Marine Corp. Many Marines were getting killed there daily. This information I was giving them was vital to getting the terrorists behind these battles. Since Fallujah and Ramadi had been evacuated due to the war going on there, the Intelligence officers didn't have much intelligence to go off of. These intelligence officers were doing everything they could to protect the Marines there, but the leads were few and far between. So once they heard about me and the colonel they flew from the Ramadi/Fallujah area to the green zone. The al-Dulaimi tribe was 95 percent ex-Iraqi Military from Saddam's time and held all kinds of high positions in Saddam's administration. This was a dangerous tribe and they were causing a lot of trouble. So as the female intelligence officer and I were making connections and working together she asked me, "Would you be interested in working for us? Your job would be to make sure Arlington Cemetery doesn't get filled up."

So I replied, "I work for LTC Burke and LT Faler, but I would do whatever is needed to protect them and others."

She said, "I understand your concern but we are a different level of intelligence and we would do what is necessary to protect you."

At this particular time this female intelligence agent didn't have a lot of information to go off of. The terrorists would come in to Fallujah and Ramadi, start a battle, kill as many Marines as they could and pull back and disappear. They would disappear like ghosts. They would go back to their villages where the buildings were made out of mud. The problem with mud villages is there are all kinds of tunnel networks under the village. The Marines would go in to fight and get these guys, but the terrorists would disappear. I have been there and I know how hard it is to operate in these mud villages with intelligence because the people disappear into thin air. These tunnels would go for miles, not just from one building to the next. This would increase the level of difficulty in trying to fight these bastards.

The female intelligence agent asked me to work for her because I could get into areas most Americans couldn't get into. A blonde haired guy with blue eyes would never be able to get into the areas I could. There was a lot of information needed and some of the best information was the street intelligence. This is the insider information of the true goings on. It's not hints, it's the actual events and movements the terrorists are planning and carrying out. You are not fighting an enemy who has a lot of technology. There was no technology to tap or hack. More often than not, the whole entire terrorist cell would only have one laptop and it would be in the lead guy's possession. So getting to the laptop would be next to impossible. So the street intelligence was the best source for leads. Even though there were main guys the Americans were looking for, finding them was a whole other ball game. You had to be able to speak to others to find out where they were hiding. This is where I would come in. I would be able to get information from the street which the intelligence agents couldn't get. They had an old data base from Saddam times. This database contained Saddam's al Fedayeen and his intelligence agents. These were the guys who were behind a lot of the terrorism the American military were fighting in the Fallujah/Ramadi area. But, these guys would change their names, look different and move locations. It was a lot of work and we had a lot of work ahead of us.

At the time, after she asked me to work for her, I looked at her and said, "I am happy to help you guys. At this point in time I have nothing to lose helping you. I am for sure at some point the terrorists will catch up to me and I don't think you can protect a dead man! I know I am wanted by them but I will do my best to get you everything you need, and if something should happen to me you can always use my PSD team." At the end I did give her information on a couple of my PSD guys, so in case I was killed she could get in touch with them.

A little after our meeting I started working for her and the U.S. intelligence agencies. She gave me all her contact information so I could reach her anywhere and anytime, but she never gave me her name. Even LT Faler didn't know her name.

Fallujah/Ramadi

When they took me back to the MOD after working with them I went straight to the personnel department inside. I had a friend who worked in the department and I asked her to pull Sabbah's MOD card for me. She was able to pull up his full name, age and blood type. Because back in Saddam's time the officers went by last name, tribal name and blood type. I also found out Sabbah was from a village called Albu Salah, which is south west of Fallujah. This village was one of the most dangerous villages and had the most dangerous killers in all Fallujah. The village was known as "The Marine Hunters or Killers" by the rest of the Ramadi tribes. Now everything was coming together for me. It made sense to me why the intelligence officer needed all the information I could give her. I got the requested information back to my intelligence contact as quick as I could. Now they had the right information so they could do their research. The intelligence officer cross-referenced the old Saddam database, they made connections and a match was made. Sabbah ended up being one of the biggest targets for the U.S. Sabbah also ended up being one of the heads, if not the head of the "Marine Killers." The intelligence officer asked me to watch all of Sabbah's steps. They were trying to figure out when Sabbah would leave the MOD for two weeks and come back. They would not initiate anything with Sabbah until he left to go home. I had every one of my soldier's watching Sabbah's every move and reporting back to me. The intelligence officers wanted to get Sabbah in his home town because it would make a huge difference in the battle against the Marines.

Sabbah had an entourage who went with him everywhere. Those men in his entourage lived in the same village as Sabbah. So the timing had to be perfect. They wanted to get Sabbah where he lived. It was easier for the intelligence team to get Sabbah where he lived because they had a full team and bigger presence in the Fallujah and Ramadi area, and it would make a bigger impact in the war. They wanted all the information on Sabbah if possible. Did Sabbah have hostages there? What kind of guns and weapons did Sabah have? How many people were in his entourage and who were they? Where in the Fallujah area were they from? All this information was needed if they were going to get Sabbah.

Fallujah and Ramadi were very important areas for the intelligence officers I was now working with. The reason those areas were so important was because of the Al Anbar campaign. This was a war in Anbar Province. The fighting that was going on was between the U.S. and Iraqi military forces and the Sunni insurgents. The war lasted for around eight years but the greatest anti-insurgence movement took place between April 2004 and September 2007. There was constant heavy fighting between the U.S. Marines and the insurgents. The insurgents started ambushing the Americans and Iraqis with IEDs. Around 9,000 Iraqi soldiers and 1,300 Americans were killed during this operation.

My guys, were still very nervous about what we had done. Even with all the intelligence work we were doing, they were still very nervous and didn't feel safe at all. They would argue a lot between each other because of their nerves and they would look at me and say, "They're coming for us, and we're fucking dead!"

One of my PSD guys looked at the rest of them and said, "We are all going to die no matter what, we will pay the price somewhere, but at least this way we kicked them in the balls."

To make everyone feel a little better we decided to change our sleeping arrangements and location. We looked at everyone as a suicide bomber and expected a suicide bomber to come for me. We were always on high alert. I didn't step foot out at the check point for a while. They were on us and we could tell by their faces they were watching me. My PSD team and I made a promise to each other we would never go home. I had never gone home since the day I joined the military. However, my PSD team guys who lived down south would go home every 2 to 3 months. I had them do this so they wouldn't get killed on their way home, or have their families killed once their homes were identified. I was sure assassins were put in place for us once we stepped off the base.

My Captain

After making my PSD guys promise me they would not go home, my captain said to me he was going to step out for a few minutes to go see his wife and kids. He hadn't been home in months, he missed them and he wanted to see them for a quick 15 minutes. He was assassinated 10 minutes after he left our base. My captain never got home to see his family and he never went home again. This had proven what I was afraid of. Even though he was not part of the PSD team or what went down the night I saved the Colonel they wanted to get someone who was close to me and make an example out of them. I never went home. Once I joined the army I knew going home wasn't an option anymore, and this supported the reason why I never went home. If the terrorists couldn't get me they would follow me to where my family was and kill them. Many people in the Iraqi military, all ranks, lost their lives and many of their families lives this way.

Sabbah is out of here

One day we noticed a shift change in the Minister of Defense's personal security detail. As we were watching

Sabbah, we noticed he and his entourage were getting ready to leave. My guys and I started taking pictures, we got license plate numbers and all the information we needed to give to the intelligence officers. I called the female intelligence officer and told her, "We have to meet today." The line I was calling her on was unsecure so I had to speak in code. I was breathing heavy and my heart was racing because I had run to call her once I saw all this movement taking place. She could tell I didn't sound like my normal self and asked me, "Are you ok?"

I told her, "Yes I'm fine, but a bird is about to fly!"

She realized it was serious and she said, "I'll be right there!"

We met at the same usual location inside the green zone away from the MOD. I handed her all the information I had which was pictures, vehicle descriptions and personal descriptions. It was pretty hard for me to get personal pictures of them. We had to pretend the PSD guys were taking pictures of each other with Sabbah's guys in the back ground.

The intelligence officer looked at me and said, "You won't hear from me for a few days, but I'll see you soon though!" She gave me a little smirk and she was gone.

As time moved on staff changes happened again at the MOD. The new officers coming in were talking about how some unknown special force teams came in and grabbed Sabbah in his village. Sabbah and a few of his men were picked up and no one knows where they were taken. All I knew was Sabbah was gone! The next time I met with the Intelligence officer I asked her, "What happened to Sabbah?"

She replied, "You don't need to worry about Sabbah anymore," as she smirked and laughed.

After Sabbah and his guys were taken out there was a large vacancy in the MOD. What was funny was that Minister al Dulaimi never said one word about it. He never talked to the Americans about it. He never asked about what happened or why Sabbah didn't come back. He kept his mouth shut because he knew what most likely happened and he didn't want to reveal he had ties to Sabbah. As far as I was concerned there was one down and many more to go! I was happy to see with the information I gave the intelligence officer, we were able to get rid of another piece of shit and save some American lives. Every time I thought about the Marines losing their lives to fighting these shit people, I always thought about my mentor, Marine Gunnery Instructor, Kevin Smalling. My PSD team was always motivated to help get the intel needed to protect the Marines. They trained us, and our PSD team always felt a special bond to them.

In the fall of 2005, after all the Sabbah stuff had quieted down, the Americans had started to evaluate their safety and potential threats which could come up in both the MOD and the MNSTC-I. Having the colonel almost kidnapped opened up many safety issues for the Americans. The Americans expected something to happen because of the people they were working around, and what happened in the MOD shook them up. When all these corrupt individuals started showing up I felt the MOD was a wild card. Because anything could happen and I kept warning LTC Burke about this. I explained to him many times not to trust the Iraqis. Many people had two faces and couldn't be trusted.

It had become a priority for the Americans to enhance their anti-terrorism preparation and training. Many situations had come up which the Americans didn't feel prepared for because the situations had not been anticipated. So a Major in the MNSTC-I had nominated me to attend this training. I was the first Iraqi ever selected to go to a special course offered by the U.S military. It was an Anti-terrorism First Protection Level 2 course. Word had gotten around with the Americans about what I had done to save the officer and they felt I would be a good candidate for this course. I was sent to this training with two other American advisors. The two other advisors were doing this higher level protection course for the MNSTC-I. They figured it would be a good opportunity for me to learn more protection techniques which I could utilize in the MOD. I had a huge responsibility in the

MOD to protect higher level American advisors, Ambassadors from other countries, including the U.S. Ambassador and Foreign Ministers of Defense. The people who would come in and out of the MOD were higher ranking people. Petraeus would come into the MOD every day and when he finished his tour he was replaced by General Dempsey. So then I had Dempsey everyday coming in and out of the MOD. It was an elite level of world officers and it was my full responsibility to protect each and every one of them. So when the course came around I was the top choice from the Iraqi side to be sent because of everything I had done. I was still continuing to work with the intelligence agents and I figured this information would help. This class was a NATO school course. When I got there I met soldiers from all over the world. There were Polish, Italians, Ecuadorians, Americans and representation from other countries too. We all slept in a tent together. It was an amazing experience. It was so cool to spend time with these soldiers and learn more about their countries, what terrorist threats they had encountered and what their country's safety concerns were. We were all excited to learn these new techniques and bring them back to our country so we could utilize them and protect our military. The course was taught by high level instructors from the U.S. Military. It introduced new information for protection and unique training tactics. These were new tactics being introduced for the first time to everyone in the classroom. The point of the class was to identify what could be done to lower the number of casualties in the military. It was learning and understanding the type of attacks terrorists would use. Terrorists would use Katyucha rockets, car bombs, suicide bombers, mortar attacks and other weapons. A good portion of these types of attacks were new for the U.S. in Iraq and tactics had to be created to protect the military personnel. We went over what type of damage each weapon could cause and what could be done to lessen the damage and deaths. One possible solution was putting metal in blocks used to build buildings so if a car bomb went off the building wouldn't collapse. They also came up with metal curtains to protect the windows. So if the windows blew the glass would not shatter and injure people. Many military personnel had been lost to these causes and something needed to be done for prevention.

The Good Ones are Gone

It was now 2006 and LTC John Burke was going to be heading back to the U.S. because his tour was ending. A new replacement came in and I continued working for the two replacements after LTC Burke. It became a job for me to escort all these people and go out on missions with them. These new lieutenant colonels coming in weren't like LTC John Burke, and they didn't understand how ugly some of the officers in the MOD were. If this wasn't bad enough, now more corrupt people were being brought into the MOD to fill different positions. These new U.S. officers were lost with these new Iraqi officials. I could trust LTC Burke but I couldn't trust many Americans at all. LTC Burke and LT Faler were worried for my life when I gave them information and never exposed me. These new guys didn't understand the position I put myself in when I gave intelligence information. They didn't understand how my life was at stake. I continued to work with them but I only did missions in the red zone with them. My communication with the intelligence officers was always kept classified. My job at the time was to protect every American's life within the MOD. My PSD guys and I put our lives on the line to protect LTC Burke and his team. What Burke didn't know was how hated he was by the Iraqi MOD officers, because he was smart and understood how they worked.

Agent X

Every day people would come to the check point and ask to speak to me. I was standing out at my check point and I see this blonde hair guy come walking over to me. He had on civilian clothes, body armor and a gun. He looked pretty sharp. He came out of the green zone gate and he walked right over to me like he knew who I was. I had never seen this guy before. He preceded to tell me his AC was broken and he was waiting for someone to come in to fix his AC. He kept talking to me and asking me questions trying to get to know me. He asked personal as well as business questions. After a couple of hours of him talking to me I asked him, "Is your AC guy coming or what? Maybe you should call him!"

He replied back, "I'm not too worried about him!"

He spoke some Arabic, he seemed pretty smart and he claimed he worked for the state department. It was about this time I realized there was no AC guy coming, he was here for another reason. At the time there was an American Soldier at the check point to the green zone. He walked over and asked this guy who he was because his badge was turned around so it couldn't been seen. Every American had a badge and the badge had to be issued by the Department of Defense. The soldier was trying to be a smart ass by questioning him. This guy respond by pulling out a black badge which not too many people carry around the green zone. The American soldier apologized and backed up. This got me concerned but it also peaked my interest because the badge he had was only carried by intelligence people, Navy SEALS or Special Forces personnel. I asked him if he was a Navy SEAL after seeing the badge.

He replied, "I use to be!" So now it made a little sense as to why he had the badge.

He had come back to my check point a few more times after this to talk to me and ask me questions. My PSD team called him "the pretty guy." I took him around the MOD. I introduced him to my PSD team and my commanding officers. He had seen all of my base and I walked him through the entire MOD to show him how we operated. After I showed him everything I asked him again who he worked for. He smiled at me and laughed. The questions he would ask were not normal questions. He was fishing for valuable information. This led me to believe he was more than a Navy SEAL. The guy was very smart and he had a pretty good idea of our Iraqi Government structure. He knew all the names of the Iraqi assassins. He knew more than anyone I had met before. He was such a unique guy and I would still ask him time and time again who he worked for. His only answer back to me was he was civil affairs and he worked for the state department. I told him "Bullshit!" He started to laugh hard. I told him straight up, "You're CIA!" He laughed and denied it. I knew it though, because I had dealt with all kinds of intelligence people from the U.S. and he was different. He was a much higher level. He and I became friends. I didn't care who he was as long as the information I gave him saved lives. I gave him all the information he wanted to know and took him to all the places he wanted to see. He was the only American who would go with me alone to places which no other Americans would go to. He visited me daily and he would spend hours with me. The stuff and information he was looking for was different from the other intelligence agents. The level of information this guy was looking for was much more in depth compared to the intelligence people I was working for. I made sure I gave him the best stuff. I even took him for a lunch with five high Iraqi officials who gave him in depth explanations of the corruption going on and who was behind it. One contractor explained to him how the money with contracts would get split by the Iraqi side. I took him in so deep he got information no other American would have been exposed to.

The corruption in the Iraqi government I showed him, educated him on, and he witnessed himself, is the unfortunate reason why Iraq has fallen apart in recent months. These higher Iraqi leaders were doing nothing but ripping off the country. And there was only so much we could do about it. No one can change the mindset of this older generation from Saddam times. This whole older generation was taught by Saddam how to steal, kill and lie. They and their conscience felt it was okay for them to do this for their own benefit. They acted like they were doing nothing wrong. These Iraqi leaders were behind a lot of shit. They stole money which was for the good of the country and many people lost their lives, both Iraqi and American military because of their greed and their desire to take control again. We found out a few of the Iraqi Army leaders were sending Iraqi soldiers to kick people out of their homes so they could rent them to someone else and make money out of it. All the corruption was driven by money and how much money they could gain.

I had come across a case involving the logistics department in the Iraqi MOD. The logistics department had been stealing millions of dollars by pretending to purchase high quality body armor for the soldiers. The soldiers never got any of this high quality body armor. They were given low quality stuff. Many of my soldiers, and I had two thousand soldiers under me, were dying every day because of this. There were so many battles going on you didn't know who the hell to fight first. The terrorists or the corrupt pieces of shit running this country. Imagine yourself fighting two different battles every day. In one battle you are getting shot in the front and the other you are getting stabbed in the back.

The thing which bothered me the most was how the government corruptness fueled and supported the terrorists in the field, and how the field terrorists worked with the government. These corrupt government officials were part of these terrorist tribes in the field. There were so many people killed and hurt for no good reason. It was all for money. I walked over millions of dollars on the floor in Saddam's palace. I never touched one dollar of it. The money was blood money. Good people died for him to get the money. I believed nothing would come good from it. Today most of these corrupt officials have taken their money and run to other countries to live their lives, while families cry every day for their lost loved ones.

Here are a couple of quotes from the Ex-Navy Seal/Intelligence Agent X. This is what he stated about our time working together and the intelligence information I gave him and how valuable the information was:

Being an America and hanging around an Iraq check point asking questions in non-existent Arabic is a good way to attract attention. In this case good attention, leaving your terps behind and not speaking much of the language can make it hard to hold a meaningful conversation. Then who enters, the youngest looking highest ranking Iraqi I have ever seen and bonus he speaks pretty damn good English. The first thing that struck me about Hamody was his positive bearing. Here was a guy who wanted to make a difference and who would make your day a little brighter in the process.

I gave him the usual line about being state department and another line of bullshit about waiting for a guy to fix the air conditioning or some such thing. I had the state department stick down pretty well when I needed a reasonable explanation for being in odd places. Of course we both knew that anyone who shows up to hang around and start conversations is automatically going to be suspected of an intelligence guy. It's like don't ask don't tell, but you want the hint of suspicion that your connected to power. With the, "I am acting like a spy but pretending not to be," established, we could start into the next phase of contemplations....what can I get out of you. Having played the game before, one expects they are going to tell you what they think you want to hear. My nice guy way involved telling them stories of working with Sunni and Shiite units with a few comments about Iraq politics, establishing I am not a cherry new guy and I know a thing or two about the chess board. I would then ask them leading questions about their motivations for what they were doing. My goals were to get their opinions on general issues and then get their first-hand knowledge of whatever specialty they might have. The tertiary goal is getting dirt on their enemies...all this makes for good trading information and depth of knowledge for the next conversation.

Hamody's responses where genuine. He was the kind of guy who gives you another reason to fight the good fight and keep working solutions for Iraq. It could be pretty frustrating dealing with the "first hustler types." With guys like Hamody you could see Iraq having potential.

Hamody didn't know it at the time, but my side project was collecting low level information of goings on of the MOI, MOD, as well as general attitude of guys on the street. I had a weekly meeting with one of the guys who put the presidential de-brief together. I never knew what he used of my information...but I think I got some new perspectives for him.

I relayed the corruption information to my friends and introduced him to a colleague...he can tell that story, I think his commanding officers had some potentially interesting info on internal affairs of MOD, I am not sure how my colleague de-conflicted with DIA but I think they probably had some kind of hand off. It's sad to see Iraq in its current state, but I am glad a few of the patriots could make it out. So many other honorable Iraqis have since died, sold out, were assassinated or abandoned by a country they called friend.

Ex-Navy Seal / Intelligence Agent X

Here is another quote from Agent X:

My first conversation I was trying to get a feel for Hamody and a general feel for his unit as well as the general goings on. We told him about my experiences with other Iraqi military and police units as well as negotiating contracts for Iraq services to U.S. forces.

The very low level scams would be Iraqi merchants overpricing goods to U.S. forces. Many times the units buying the goods had no idea what they were paying for...or naively felt they were helping out the economy and building rapport by overpaying...I on the other hand believe they were making the U.S. look like a bunch of suckers, ready to fall for a great many scams. This undercut U.S. authority and prestige in larger political and military stabilization efforts as the naivety to a native observer was rather plain. I believe this kind of careless attitude and culture that U.S. units portrayed only emboldened corruption schemes in the Iraqi military. Because in many cases the corruption was so easy and so profitable, many people's attitude was that one was an idiot for not taking advantages where one could.

With this in mind I talked to Hamody and basically let him know I was concerned about U.S. forces getting suckered by these many schemes. Between hanging out with Hamody and his unit, he started telling me about one of the scams that was

*currently going on, where Iraq officers in charge of logistics
would take the money allocated for high quality body armor,
helmets, boots and combat uniforms. To replace the high
quality gear they would take a small fraction of the stolen
money and buy outdated or damaged goods to still make
payroll.*

*I think with my positive response to these revelations
and my assurance that I would pass on the information to
proper authorities he introduced me to. I do remember them
telling me about some kind of bad actors and remember asking
them questions to try and get an idea if these were merely rivals
they wanted help getting rid of or true enemies.*

*I turned the investigation of potential enemy actors in
MOD over to another unit. I think ultimately they deconflicted
this with DIA and allowed DIA to continue the case from there.
At this point I didn't have a whole lot of close contact, as I
needed to keep some kind of cover established.*

*Another memorable meeting with Hamody was him
detailing the practice of an MOD unit utilizing their soldiers to
act as slumlords and strong-arm rent collectors. A number of
weeks after my first meeting with Hamody, I again stopped by
and had lunch/dinner with him. He started telling me about
how some of the units were raiding houses and kicking people
out and or arresting them. They would then go to another house
on the list and shake the occupants down for rent money.
Apparently this had turned into a full-time job for the Iraqi*

military unit. With little oversight or a "look the other way" understanding among similar military units, a commander could run a number of "side businesses." This made the significant sums of money for the officers. If an officer wasn't into some kind of side business he would be targeted by the others as he would highlight their wrong-doing and could potentially bring some kind of justice on the wrong-doers. This kind of pressure really put a lot of pressure on potentially good Iraqi officers.

I had seen a LOT of the ghost soldier tricks and Hamody confirmed it was also a problem in units that he had seen. Because it was so widespread and there was no well thought out plan for stopping the practice, nothing significant was done about this at the time.

These corruption practices can easily be seen as a significant contribution to the weakness of the Iraqi army and the rise of ISIL in Northern Iraq. Unfortunately an overall plan for correcting the corruption culture was not established so there was little well-meaning soldiers could do to stop it and those who tried truly took large risks in doing so.

Hamody's talks would many times confirm trends I was seeing and his detailed explanations of goings on in the MOD would let me build a better picture and understanding, which was invaluable in working with MOI police, U.S. Department of State and assorted U.S. military / intelligence units.

A few of his stories ended up making it into my informal weekly debriefings with one of the direct presidential advisors. At the time the advisor was very interested in atmospheric and street level intelligence and found my and Hamody's information valuable. As to what and how this was briefed to the president I do not know. But he was always eager to meet on Wednesday afternoons.

Ex-Navy Seal / Intelligence Officer X

11

Suicide Belt

Now let's not forget I did piss off the biggest terrorist organizations in the world, al Qaeda and the Islamic State in Iraq. I did defeat their plans to take American lives. These Americans were here to better our country and they didn't deserve to be hurt or killed. The terrorist's motive was to scare the Americans so they would leave the MOD and give control back to the corrupt government. But trust me, these terrorist organizations had more up their sleeves. The al-Qaeda members working in the MOD tried their best to use the Iraqi government influence to get me out of my position. They would put in complaints against me and my guys. They would send people to enter the MOD through the exit and not the entrance. When civilian vehicles and MOD employees tried to come in through the exit and give us a hard time, we had to treat them like suicide bombers, so our instructions were to shoot at them. A complaint had been filed stating my soldiers and I had shot at a vehicle coming in through an exit.

The idea behind filing the complaint was so the complaint would find its way up to the higher officials so I could be fired and removed from the check point. Once the complaint reached the higher officials, an investigation would open. Their plan was to get me fired and upon leaving the MOD, al Qaeda would execute me. I knew how to get the right people involved.

Zebari

At the time, I got the Primary Chairman of the Joint Chiefs of Staff involved, Babaker Zebari. Zebari was from a Kurdish back ground. He was a professional soldier back in the day, and he was a good guy. In his position, he made sure the Iraqi army would never assault the Kurds the way they did back in the 1980s. Today he is the new leader of the Iraqi Army. He is the highest ranking officer in the military. At the time, he looked at the complaint, investigated it and he took my side. Zebari was a soldier and he was also a Kurd. He understood what they were trying to do. He told me I was fine and to go back and keep doing my job.

I continued to work with the U.S. intelligence officers. I had so much motivation to give them the information they needed. I wanted nothing more than to see these bastards get taken down. Every day there would be a black sign on the front of the MOD with someones name on it. This was a tradition where if someone died, or was killed, their name would be displayed on this sign. The assassinations were rampant. The terrorists kept killing good people. They were killing anyone who they didn't want in the MOD.

One afternoon I am sitting at my check point and guns start to fire towards us from inside the MOD. The bullets were flying over my head at the check point. I ran into the MOD to find out what was going on. I found my PSD team shooting from the window of the office of General Naseer al Abadi. A sniper had taken a shot at the general while he was sitting at his desk inside the MOD. The amount of effort put in to assassinate him had hit a new level. They shot at him from the top of a Marriott Hotel which was a distance away. The calculations this sniper used had a lot of planning put into it. This was a new type of attack on the MOD. After this, General al Abadi retired. He didn't want his name on the front of the MOD and the list of dead people. He was a good guy and he would have been the future of the Iraqi Military. This was the first of many assassination attempts inside the MOD.

There were some new guys coming through my check point and they looked very suspect to me. I started using the British company more and more to search these guys more thoroughly. I had a lot of political pressure on me which prevented me from doing my job. I myself wanted to search these guys but I couldn't. So by using the British company, there were no political ties to the Iraqi government and there was nothing they could say or do against them. There was a lot of new activity going on at my check point. I saw a lot of new faces coming into the MOD many of whom I was not familiar with. But it made sense to me seeing these new faces because the terrorists in the MOD were trying to bring in more and more of their people. The terrorists wanted to control and nominate the people they wanted to run the MOD. If there was a position open in the MOD and there were six guys for the job, the one good guy would be assassinated and the position would go to one of the bad guys. The terrorists had a goal to take control of the leadership and lead the military.

This was evident to me back when I had started working in the military. I remember listening to a meeting back in 2004 between an American colonel and the higher Iraqi military personnel. This colonel was smart and had a good pulse on these guys. His first question to them was to ask what weapons would their new military need. The Iraqi leaders answered back by listing rockets and ammunition which would go through armored vehicles. The colonel shook his head in agreement of acknowledgement as he listened to them, stood up and said to them "And this is what you will use to get the Americans out of Iraq?" The Iraqi officials were in shock and denied it. The colonel stood up, looked at them and in a matter of a few words told them to go fuck themselves. It was classic. It was the best thing I had ever seen or heard. The Iraqi officials were so befuddled they didn't know what to say.

The sad truth was the Iraqis did want to get the Americans out of the MOD. Remember LTC Burke had General Mohan red listed after the death of General Ayad. Mohan was not allowed to take any positions or be in any meetings because there were so many questions about him. Trust me he still held his secret meetings outside the MOD. The terrorists who worked and were loyal to Mohan wanted to figure out a way to scare the Americans so the American advisors would pull out of the MOD and not be involved in there anymore. It was revenge for what LTC Burke had done to Mohan. General Mohan even though he was red listed in the MOD could still carry out his political agendas with his own political party. He could come up with plans and have his loyal posse carry it out in the MOD. I had gotten some Iraqi intelligence information informing us something was going to go on inside the MOD, but we didn't know when or where it would take place. After receiving this information I decided I had to increase the level of security in the MOD. I was going to need eyes everywhere inside the building. I brought more MP guys into the MOD. I had one in and on every corner of the MOD. Also, I had to search these guys coming in and out of my check point. The only device I had was a metal detecting device. I had no other technology, no trained canines and nothing to detect C4 or any type of explosive and the terrorists knew this. My only extra defense was this British company to search them. I was worried something big was going to go down and I needed to figure it out fast.

The U.S. intelligence officers I had been working with were finishing up their tour and going home. A new team of Intelligence officers had come in and were informed on my working relationship with them. I explained to the new intelligence agents what I felt was going on inside the MOD. They told me as these guys went through my check point every day I was to verify them, get to know them better and keep a close eye on them.

Ziyad is up to something

Days passed and nothing had happened yet, which gave me a bad feeling. I would stand at my check point and watch my guys and the British security guys search people coming in to the MOD. So one day I see this guy, Colonel Ziyad who worked in the Iraqi operations center, being searched. He had a smile on his face as he was being searched which made no sense. This guy was an old Ba'athist and he was from the Fallujah area. He had a lot of mystery to him and he was the one who yelled at me in front of LTC Burke about why I was inside the operations center. These old regime guys had a lot of games they would play. Searching them was not my best defense at all, but it was all I had and could do. His bizarre behavior at the check point made me feel we needed to start watching him more. His face and smile looked as though he was in the middle of doing something and we weren't smart enough to pick up on it. Inside the MOD operations center each officer had a locker. The lockers were in a separate room near the entrance of the operations center. One of my military police happened to guard this room. Using him I was able to walk into the locker room and identify which locker belonged to Ziyad and his friends.

The locker had a lock on it. I took a picture of the lock and I found many locks in the Iraqi markets which looked the exact same. I went and bought a new lock. I could relock the locker with it after I opened it. This way Ziyad wouldn't realize someone searched his locker, and think his key didn't work and get a new lock. The keys not working was a common issue and wouldn't tip him off. I was advised to do this by the American intelligence people I was working with. I picked up a new lock and went back. My military police officer was so nervous about me doing this. He begged me to never tell anyone about this. He had a wife and children and he didn't want anything to happen to him or them. He also didn't want to lose his job over this either. I explained to him if there was something bad going on in there, chances are he would be going down with it or getting killed. I had no idea if anything was in the locker. It was a complete shot in the dark, but my gut told me to check it. I made a plan as to when and how I was going to go do it.

Opening the Locker

I went back after work hours, after Ziyad left the gate. I had to be careful as I entered this room because some of Ziyad's guys could still be around in the operations center. I took a lock cutter with me and I cut the lock. I was so nervous I could feel my heart beating in my throat. If I was caught doing this I would most likely lose my job and after be killed by Ziyad's guys. As I opened the locker there was a uniform hanging in front of me. It was Ziyad's work uniform. I moved the uniform to the side to look deeper inside. Behind the uniform there was a big black bag which was shoved in the back of the locker. All I could think was, "Fuck, there is nothing here!" My MP Officer kept pressuring me to leave because there was nothing there. I said, "Fuck it, I'm opening the bag." I had come too far now to walk away. I pulled the bag out because it was dark inside the locker and I opened the bag. Inside the bag I saw a military belt with a bunch of wires attached to it. I was like, "What the hell is this!" With extreme caution, I pulled the military belt out to look at it. I discovered it was a military belt filled with explosives and wires attached to it. It was a suicide belt. The belt looked like it was still being built and was in the process of being finished. My big question was how the hell were they getting explosives into the MOD. We were searching them as best we could. My military police officer was shocked and had nothing to say. Based upon what we found in the black bag with the suicide belt we figured out explosives were being brought into the MOD inside cigarettes. Under the filter of the cigarette the tobacco had been replaced with explosives. Nobody would ever think to check the cigarettes, and even a small amount of explosive can be damaging. Ziyad had been bringing in small amounts of explosives for a long time mixed in his cigarette box and we never noticed. After this discovery and to this day, the MOD check point does not allow cigarettes or cigars to enter MOD.

I told my MP guy not to move and all I could think was, "I did it again! I am a fucking dead man."

Sabbah's guys were nowhere near as capable and ruthless as Mohan and Ziyad's guys were. Mohan's guys had bigger long term goals to take over and be in charge. They wanted the Americans out from being involved in the Iraqi leadership. Sabbah's guys were people who wanted to fight and kill Americans. They had no big goals. This suicide belt was in retaliation to LTC Burke and his team. By LTC Burke red-listing Mohan, this delayed him and his guys from taking over the Iraqi Military. This suicide belt was made to change the American Policy in the MOD. If the belt had gone off and killed a few Americans, this would have been a victory for Mohan and his guys. Because the Americans would have pulled every Adviser out of the MOD leaving the Iraqis to take control.

I still was in disbelief as to what I had just done and what I had found. My heart sank. I was so relieved to find it and yet I was so mad at myself. I went and hit the emergency button in the hall way to alert all my troops inside the MOD and total chaos broke out. I knew by the time Ziyad's guys inside the MOD called him they would be ready to kill me.

There was an address listed in the data base for Ziyad. I got a patrol together and my patrol and I went to the address listed to find him. When we got there, it was obvious Ziyad had gotten a call, because there was not one person in the apartment. This meant some of Ziyad's guys were in the operations center tonight. Everything in the apartment was like they were still there, but we had just missed them by a few minutes. There was still hot tea sitting on the stove. Ziyad had gotten a call and ran.

I Have Two Strikes Now

When I got back to the MOD and the operations center after going to Ziyad's apartment, the officers there told me "good job." But all I could think about was my mom when officers went to notify her I had died. I knew I had gone too far this time. I went too deep and I didn't know how the hell I was getting out of this. The U.S. intelligence agents I was working with at the time were very happy with my accomplishment. I had gone above and beyond what anyone had ever done before. This was a great victory, but I was more worried about my life. At this moment I didn't feel like there was any way out. So I figured I was a dead man and if I was going to die, I wanted to at least die in uniform. For my safety the U.S. Intelligence officers hooked me up by giving me ID cards which would let me into the green zone. Those ID's allowed me into (Forward Operating Base) FOB Prosperity, which was a large U.S. military base, and to any other military base in Iraq. From that night on, I only slept there. I knew if I stayed in the MOD they would without a doubt kill me. After all this going down I would work during the day at the MOD and after I would go back to the green zone every night to sleep. I had reached a new point with the terrorists in the MOD. I knew at some point they would figure out a way to get to me, but I didn't care. So I decided I was going to keep fighting them regardless of what could happen because I hated them so much.

12

Negotiating with Terrorists

At my MOD checkpoint post I would sit in my office every day and survey people coming to the check point. Iraqi citizens would come to my check point all the time to find their loved ones who had died. When an Iraqi soldier from any unit in the country died, his body would be most likely be brought to the U.S. combat hospital in the green zone. I had volunteered at the time to go get the dead bodies from the hospital because I could get into the green zone. The families wanted the body of their loved one so they could lay them to rest. So I would go get the body and meet the family at the gate. I did this because one of those dead bodies happened to be my cousin. My mother's sister lost her son. He was being harassed by the terrorists in the neighborhood. He didn't want anything to do with them so they killed him. They bound his hands with wire and shot him in the head. Do you know how hard it is to bring the body of a close family member to your mother and family, and not show any emotions because you don't want anyone knowing they're family? It was so tough and it broke my heart that I had to act this way, but I didn't want to risk their lives. The corrupt people in the MOD would have loved to see my family and follow them home. I can guarantee they would have gotten to them one way or another and my family didn't need anything extra after going through this.

One of my soldiers came to me one day and told me there was a woman at the gate telling them her son had been kidnapped. The people who took him wanted money and she needed help. They wanted twenty thousand dollars for her son at the time. I went out to speak to her. She was devastated and crying. She had gone to the police, the Americans and anyone else she could think of. It was an unknown car which had picked him up with a group of people wearing covers over their faces. She had nothing to sell to get the money. She had no way of getting that money. She kept begging me to help her. I told her I would try to do what I could. I had felt so bad for my aunt losing her son and this woman reminded me of her. I wanted to help this lady so I started asking her more questions. I asked her if she knew of anyone in her area who was bad or maybe a terrorist. She said she knew of one guy who was most likely behind this. She told me more about the guy. This guy had money but he didn't have a job. Kidnapping happened to be a fundraiser for terrorists. So I gathered my PSD team and I told them about this mother. My PSD team at the time would help me when something needed to be done under cover. We were brothers and we trusted each other with our lives. I told them this was a volunteer operation and the Iraqi military should not know about this. At first my PSD team was against doing this. This lady happened to live in a tough neighborhood. As a team we were either all in together to do the mission or not. So I told the team to please go speak with the mother, and if they still felt the same way we wouldn't do the mission. I had a picture of the kid, and my team had gotten more information from the mom. After the rest of the PSD team spoke to the mom and saw how desperate she was, the mission was a go.

There was a fair amount of preparation for us before we went out on these low-profile missions. We would research the village or neighborhood. We would go on Myspace and see if we could get better pictures of the suspect, personal information and what we could use as a possible weakness. Myspace was hot in Iraq at the time and most of these young terrorists were on it. For us to be successful we had to know where we were going, what our potential dangers could be and what the captors looked like. Our biggest concern was how much time we had to complete the mission. Our initial plan was to go out at night and as civilians. We could not let anyone know we were military. Once we got him we would cover his eyes with a blind fold so he would not know where he was going or who we were. We would let him think up who we were. We needed to scare this bastard and tell him we were going to kill his family if he didn't tell us where the kid was. See, if we operated as the military we wouldn't be able to say this kind of stuff or make threats because we could get in trouble if we did. Terrorists had different ways they would raise money. Kidnapping people made quick cash for them. They would target people who had money. For me and my PSD team, this was about humanity and helping our people. This was not a job for us. We were happy to help her.

We decided we would go out at night. We had to go in low profile, but we had our body armor on under our civilian clothes, we had masks to cover our faces and we were armed.

Before we entered the house of the captor, I was speaking to my PSD team member. He was a member of the Iraqi military since 1979 and he read a lot of books in the battle zone. He loved reading about human psychology. He would prepare me on how to talk to these terrorists and how to break them down. Negotiating and dealing with these guys was a mental game. The best approach was to show them and make them feel we had nothing to worry about and nothing to lose. And, if we didn't get what we wanted, it would not only get ugly for them but for their families also. We had to show them we were bigger and stronger than they were and we worked for someone bigger than they were. We had to pretend we had a criminal side. We couldn't use our military side.

As we entered this guy's house we looked like criminals ourselves. We used our military training as we entered the house. We broke up into two teams. One team went into the house and the other team stayed outside the house. If my team outside told me it was time to go, we would have to pull out. We were not equipped to take on a big fire fight. If everything was going well outside, I had ten to fifteen minutes to complete the job.

I led the interrogations on this first mission at the captor's home. I sat him in a chair and pointed the gun at his family. I showed the kid's picture to him and I asked him where this kid was. I told him, "I need the kid now."

He said, "I swear I don't know!"

I told him, "I will kill your family right here if you don't tell me where this kid is." He asked me if he could make a couple of phone calls. I needed to scare him to the point where he would give me the information I needed. After he made the phone calls, he identified two individuals who had the kid in an unknown empty house. These two individuals would be our new targets. It was a good lead and a good start to getting this kid. I asked him if he knew if these two individuals, who were holding the boy, had families of their own. I told him if he gave me accurate information I will let him and his family go. If the information was no good, I would be back, but for now he was coming with us. I would have loved to kill this bastard, but I needed him alive to get this kid back. We had to think as negotiators and not as military. I was nervous, but I needed to get this kid.

I went to the first new target's house, whom we were told had the kid. He had a wife and kids of his own. We broke the door and went in the house. We took the initial guy in with us and kept him duct taped in the trunk of our car. The guy we were looking for was named Uday. The family told us he worked nights and he was working at the time. They didn't know where he worked. I asked the wife if she had a cell phone and if she contacted him often. She said yes, I got her cell phone and I called Uday. Uday answered the phone expecting his wife, but I surprised him instead. I told him "If you want to see your father, wife and kids live another day, you need to tell me where the boy is right now. If I don't get the kid, you don't get your family! You think you're a natural killer? Well you brought natural killers into your home!"

Uday responded back, "I have the kid." I told him to put the kidnapped boy on the phone to verify it was him

Uday told me, "If you let my family go, I will let the kid go."

I told him, "That's not how this works." I need to see the kid first before I let them go. I have seven members of your family and you have someone I don't even know, so we can debate this if you want. And, right now you don't want to piss me off!"

He said, "Fine!"

My PSD team took the father as collateral and we let the guy in the trunk go. I told the guy in the trunk to pray he never saw me again! I told Uday when the mother calls me telling me she has her son back I would let his father go. I also told him I didn't want him, I wanted the kid. I did warn him if he killed the boy, I would kill his whole family. We covered Uday's father's eyes, and took him back to an unknown location at our base. Uday's father had no idea his son was a terrorist or did this type of activity. Around six o'clock in the morning the mom of the kidnapped boy called my cell phone. She had her son. She also had her belongings packed up and she was ready to get her family out of the country. She was crying and could not thank me enough. She said to me, "You are magic, you saved my son, and you are like a terrorist whisperer. I thought I would never see my son again."

I told her to get out and go as far as she could. She called me an hour later to tell me she had left town. I took the father and I put him back into our car before all the MOD personnel started to come in. I told the father who I was and I told him his son was kidnapping people to raise money for terrorist purposes. I explained to him this was the only and last opportunity their family had. I told him, if I was him, I would tell my son to knock this shit off. I asked him how it felt to have guns pointed on him and to be taken from his family and that he needed to understand how it felt for others. He shook his head yes, he understood. I let him go. The PSD and I felt so accomplished that we did something good. Not one of my PSD team complained. They enjoyed helping. After this I became known with my soldiers as the negotiator and they called me the terrorist whisperer after what the mother said. I started getting more and more of these types of cases. The mother had told some people about how I saved her son. People who were desperate for help would come to my check point asking for me. I had to be careful with the people who wanted to speak to me. I was wanted by the terrorists myself and I had to be cautious about who I worked with and I was always looking over my shoulder. I always checked people out before I spoke with them to make sure it wasn't a set-up of any type.

Saving Ahmed

A few days later another case showed up. He was an Iraqi business man who owned a lot of properties. He kept asking for me. He came back a couple of times before I met him because I wasn't sure who he was. I met him one day at the check a point and he had introduced himself to me. He was desperate, his son was kidnapped. His son was twenty years old. The kidnappers wanted two hundred thousand dollars cash and he only had ninety thousand dollars cash on him. Understand even if this guy gave the kidnappers the two hundred thousand dollars there was no guarantee they would deliver the son back. He would have to sell his properties to get all of the money together and it would take time. The son was in a very dangerous position because of the time it would take to get all money together. This gentleman lived in a wealthy area, which made him and his family a clear target. He asked me to think about it and let me know. He came back the day after and he brought his wife and daughter with him. He was worried the kidnappers would abduct the rest of his family. The daughter came in and begged us. I spoke to my PSD team. I asked them to go outside and meet this family. If they didn't think we could do it, to please tell the family so we could all back out together as a team. The son's name was Ahmed and time was running out. If the terrorists didn't get the money on time, they would kill Ahmed. My PSD team and I were cautious on this case because it was the highest ransom we had worked with. This meant the terrorists had more capabilities. We decided as a team to do it. I got the information we needed from the father. He didn't know who could have taken his son. He works all day long. He showed me the phone number the terrorists called him from. The lucky break for us here was the terrorists were dumb enough to use their own cell phone. I took the number and I went to the biggest cell phone company in Iraq, called Iraqna. I went there in a military uniform and convoy. Every cell phone which was purchased had a SIM card which was registered to the purchaser. I asked Iraqna to pull this number to see who owned this phone and what store it was purchased at. It was purchased in the same town Ahmed's family resides. This was our first lead. The family kept calling me every two hours. I told the father to give me a little time to do some investigating. I explained to the father to tell the terrorists the property would be selling in a couple of days and they would have their money. I explained to him under no circumstances should he tell anyone what we were doing because it would put Ahmed's life, my PSD team and my life in jeopardy,

I sent my PSD team to go to the Iraqna store owner in the family's neighborhood. The store would have a copy of the ID of who bought the phone. This was our one little hope in the middle of the ocean. There were no other leads. If we had found out this was a stolen phone, we would have turned the case down. Two of my guys enter the store in civilian clothes. They start to talk to the store owner, but he wouldn't give them any information. My guys had to pull their guns out and once they did they got all the information they needed. The Iraqi gencia for this individual had been updated and it was a picture of some guy. They brought the picture back to the base. I had the family come down to our base to see if they could identify the guy in the picture. The daughter knew who the guy was. She had seen him in the neighborhood and he lived a few blocks away. The daughter found out for us where the guy lived. We also learned this guy had a big family, but we still had no idea where Ahmed was. The daughter and her friends started watching this guy's every move to get more information about him. One of her friends had spoken to the guy we were looking for before. He had hit on her before and gave her his cell phone number. We had her friend listen to the voice on the voice mail recordings to see if it was him. Her friend was able to identify the voice, as well as the house where his family lived. We felt good we had our guy. By the third day the kidnappers were pressuring Ahmed's dad and telling him Ahmed would be dead soon. These guys were scaring him. We told the dad and family to prepare to leave the country once we got their son. The father said he was prepared to go to Jordan and he would let his properties go.

As a team we decide to go in the middle of the night and grab the terrorist's family. If he wasn't there we would get his parents. We were raiding a terrorist's house. We knew if a fire fight broke out we would have to kill some people. Around 1 a.m. we entered the house. We zip tied his brothers and put them in one room. We woke up his parents and zip tied them. But the guy we wanted wasn't home. I felt so bad but I had to put the gun on his parents. They wouldn't tell me where their son was at the time, but I could tell by their faces they knew. I told them I wasn't there to kill their son. He had something I needed and I needed to speak with him. They called their son on his cell phone, which was the same number we had from Ahmed's father. It was now confirmed we had the right guy. His father called and spoke with him. After his father spoke with him he told us his son was sleeping at his friend's house. It happened to be a group of guys who stayed at this one house about one block away. I told the father to call him back and give the phone to me. I told this piece of shit I was about to execute his whole family in five minutes if he didn't get me what I needed. I put his mom on the phone. She told him we were armed with big guns, looked like assassins and not to come home. I hated to act so ugly to his parents. These parents, like most parents I encountered, didn't know what their kids were doing or the terrorist activities they participated in. My goal was to get Ahmed alive. I told him on the phone, "There is only one thing which will save your family and your savior right now is Ahmed."

He was silent for a second and he responded, "And?" in a real sarcastic way.

Because this guy was such a sarcastic asshole I replied back, "Or you can give me two hundred thousand dollars for your family and I am willing to bet you don't have it"... and I laughed because I was joking. I told him I knew he had Ahmed and I needed him right now.

In a much different tone of voice he asked me, "What should I do?"

I told him, "Shut the fuck up and listen! I know you're a block away. I could come right know and fuck you up myself, but I can guarantee you don't want me there. So, let Ahmed walk out right now and go home!" I didn't hear anything on the other end of the phone for a few seconds. So I told him, "I will take your parents with me and if I don't see Ahmed standing in front of his house. I will blow your parents fucking heads off in the street! So tell Ahmed to fucking run!" Little did anyone know I was shitting my pants myself! I was so nervous. We put the parents in the car and drove to Ahmed's house. I parked in front of the house. I saw a kid coming toward our car who looked like Ahmed. I got out of the car and told him I was a friend of his father. This poor kid was so frightened. I told Ahmed he needed to get in the car with me. He was so hesitant to do so. I explained to him his father and sister were waiting for him and I needed to take him to them. Ahmed's family was not staying at their house for fear of the daughter being abducted. The parents of the kidnapper were still with me. At this point I let the mother out, but I held on to the father. I called the kidnapper on the phone again. I told him, "In case you have an ambush waiting for us I want you to know I let your mom out but you will be shooting at your father."

He responded back to me, "That's not what you promised!"

I told him, "I don't make promises!" Once I drive out of town I will let your father go and he can walk home! I hope he's in good shape!" I was so thankful we had done it and we were driving back to the base with Ahmed. I called Ahmed's parents and they talked to him on the phone. I told the parents to pack their car, be ready to go and come get their son. Before we got back to the base we let the father of the kidnapper go.

My guys asked him, "When was the last time you exercised?"

He responded, "Back when I was young."

They said, "Good news. You're young again today!" As they pushed him out of the car.

When we got back to the base, Ahmed's father was there with a leather bag in his hand. He took the leather bag, grabbed my hand and put the bag's handles in my hand. I asked him, "What is this?"

He said, "Open it." The bag was full of cash.

He then said, "This is what I was going to pay for my son and I want you to have it. I don't need the money because I have my son back."

On top of the money was gold jewelry. I handed the bag back to him and I said, "Every day I am on this earth is a good day and this money won't do me any good when I am in the grave. If you could please pray for me I would appreciate that more."

It was so crazy to look at this huge amount of money. My PSD guys had never seen this much cash before. As the father and his family drove away, my very good friend on the PSD looked at me and said, "You grew ten feet in my eyes."

Meaning I was a huge person for giving the money back. But I could have never kept any of the money. The money was blood money and it would not have been right to take it.

The Terrorists Weakness

My PSD team and I continued to do more of these cases. After getting some experience with these cases I started to learn there was a point of weakness in each terrorist and each terrorist organization. I started to understand the psychology of them. We had figured out how to take them from being a monster back to a human being. My team and I figured this was a good way to protect our lives. At this point we had only done a few missions to see how successful we could be. After there were so many more private missions, we went on to help people. Some people we could help and some people we couldn't help. We did save many young individuals, but there were some we couldn't save. It got around that I was starting to be known as "The Terrorist Whisperer" because my team and I had helped so many. Having this title started to scare me more and more and I knew in the back of my mind al-Qaeda in the MOD was still planning on executing me at some point.

There is one mission I will always remember which stands out forever in my mind as the greatest takedown of a very lethal terrorist, who had the greatest weakness of all. My battalion commander at the time got an order to leave his deputy commander to go help out another battalion. My battalion headquarters was located in Al Muthana International Airport. My commander was called to go to Latifiya. Latifiya is a city south of Baghdad which had about 250,000 citizens. It was home to the 1/4/6 Iraqi Army Battalion. It was also part of the area known as "The Triangle of Death." This area was home for about one million Sunni civilians in it. It went from Baghdad to Al Hillah. It was given this name from 2003-2010 during the occupation of Iraq. This area was known for a lot of violence and killing of both American and Iraqi forces.

The call my Iraqi Commander got was an emergency call from the Iraqi Army Chief of Staff. The commander of the battalion there was killed. The Chief of Staff told my commander he had to go and take over the battalion. The commander there happened to be killed by a terrorist called "The Fox Man." The Fox Man was a known terrorist. He was one of the main leaders in the area known as The Triangle of Death. This terrorist had killed around 75 Iraqi soldiers with a sword. He would go to their homes and execute them by beheading them in front of their home and family. He terrorized all the soldiers in the area and they were afraid to report to their unit. This terrorist also had control over the local business people too. He would not allow them to sell their goods to the Iraqi soldiers and he also charged these business people a percentage of their sales which went to Al Mujahideen. Al Mujahideen was a Sunni militant group which was part of al-Qaeda and this was their fund-raiser to support their group.

When my commander got there, the battalion was in very bad shape. There were not enough soldiers there to be a battalion. My commander was nervous. He called me and asked if half of the PSD team and I could come up and support him. He told us he was going to need us for a few weeks. So half of my team and I went. The other half of the team stayed behind to watch over the MOD. Our PSD team had amazing training and he felt maybe we could help him get control over the situation up there and bring morale back to the battalion. As soon as we got there, we entered the gate and we could see the poor shape the battalion was in. There was no signs of any Iraqi soldiers patrolling. This meant the city was in complete control of the terrorists. As we sat down with my commander for our first task force meeting he started the meeting by saying, "Thank you for coming to die with me here." My commander felt hopeless at this point. Americans here were even getting hit with IEDs. No one was able to patrol the roads at all.

The Prostitute

As a group we started to come up with a plan as to how we should start fixing this problem. We had to be careful with our plan. We didn't want to go outside into the city because it was too risky. So after a few hours of discussing possibilities I asked what if we went straight for the Fox Man. My commander looked at me and said, "Sure, let's invite him to dinner!" Everyone laughed, they thought it was a crazy idea. My commander asked me what my plan was to get the Fox Man without being killed. I explained to my commander I felt he had to have a weakness of some sort. The next day I found an NCO in the battalion who had some information on the Fox Man and his movements. I found out he was single, no kids, no family and no one knew where he came from. There were so many tribes in the area they figured he must be from one of them. The more I talked to the NCO, the more I found out he had good knowledge of the area we were in. One thing which got my attention was the NCO said the Fox Man would hit on all the widows in the area. He would go and visit them and spend time with them at night. This made me feel like maybe there was a weakness there.

I went back to my commander and PSD team to discuss with them an idea I came up with. I told my commander I had figured out a weapon which could work on the Fox man. My commander said, "OK, let's hear it!"

I responded back to him, "Women!"

My commander looked at me and said, "That is impossible. The Fox is religious and he is a jihadist."

My PSD team member looked at my commander and said, "yes he is a jihadist, but his penis is not!"

We all got a good laugh, but I told them I thought it would work. There were no other weapons which could get to this guy. So, I felt going after him in a personal way would work the best.

My commander said, "You can try it, but I know nothing about this if it doesn't work. You only have a twelve thousand dollar budget for this battalion. If it works this is one for the history books and if it doesn't our battalion is broke!"

My PSD team and I figured out we had to get a good looking woman who knew how to talk to men. She had to be able to sell herself and reel him in for us. There were no women in the Iraqi Military who looked good enough, had the ability to do this or were willing to do this. My PSD team member said joking around, "We need a prostitute!"

I looked at him and said, "Perfect!"

We went to a street in Baghdad which was famous for hiring prostitutes. We faked a government letter stating we would be kicking them out of this area due to their prostitution activities. We arrived in our military convoy as a way to look more official and scare them. I ended up speaking to one of the older women who was the Madame. I told her there was a way for her to get the government to forget about this letter. I explained to her she and the other ladies had to help out the military. She was all ears now. She asked what she needed to do. I told her I was looking for a girl, and I gave her the description of the girl I was looking for. At first she thought we were looking for prostitutes. I told her we were not looking for anything we only needed a girl to help us complete a job. We told her we needed one girl who had the heart of a lion. She said, "I think I have the girl for you." She told us to wait a bit. A few minutes later she showed up with a girl in her late twenties and she was beautiful. The girl was more than what we were looking for and she carried herself very well and she was a sweet talker. She was the perfect magnet for our guy.

I started to explain to the girl what we needed her to do and she got nervous. I explained to her no matter what, we would bring her out alive and unharmed. I explained to her it was only a couple of days that we needed her. She asked how much she would be getting paid. I told her ten thousand dollars for a couple of days of work. Her jaw dropped. She agreed to do the job and we put a plan together.

We rented a civilian truck, got her some old furniture and we had her contact a real estate agent to find a house for rent in the area the Fox Man was. She went on to explain to the real estate agent she was widowed and she needed a home. He gave her a couple options and we chose the housing closest to the base. The reason for this was we needed to be able to grab the guy fast and run him back to the base as quick as we could. We didn't want to travel a far distance and risk being attacked. Two days later, the real estate agent called her back and gave her the okay. We used a civilian driver to drive her and the furniture to the new house. Our girl was from an area in Baghdad which did not have any ties with any of the tribes in this area. We were a little worried she might experience a little trouble because she was a foreigner. But, it also made her the perfect bait for the Fox Man because he would investigate a foreigner.

It was move-in day at the house and we had given her a cell phone prior to her getting there. This way she could reach us 24/7. She was at the house no longer than a day and the Fox Man showed up to check her out. She called me after he left. She explained to me she had met him and he told her he was in charge of this area. He asked her a few questions about who she was and where she was from. She answered him very seductively and pretended she was the lonely widow. As he left he gave her his personal phone number. She also explained to us that he had a few men with him when he showed up and he didn't seem to travel alone. The details she gave us we kept classified at the base for only the PSD team and I. There was no room for error at all. Our lives and this young lady's life were at stake. She called and told me the next day he had been calling her. He told her he wanted to come over and spend some time with her during the night. We told her to call him back and tell him she wasn't ready and maybe another day. We needed a day to get ready to grab him. We had only seconds to grab him. If we spent too much time there we would be in the middle of a fire fight with all the tribe members. This mission had to be an error free plan. Planned second by second. The time between the base and the house was about thirteen minutes. We had one and a half minutes to grab him, put him in the car and get out of there before anyone noticed anything. We told her to call him back and tell him to come over as late as he could. She made an arrangement with him to come over at 4 am the next morning. I told her when she hears him at the front door to call my number on her cell phone and hang up. This was a code to let me know he was there. We told her she had to keep him busy for about fifteen minutes until till we got there.

The next day came and as a team we rehearsed how we were going to grab him and run. In the middle of the day our girl called us to inform us he was going to come over around 4 am. I told her not to get nervous and to pretend he was a customer. I did explain to her she had to keep him busy for fifteen minutes until we got there. My team and I at the based got prepared and ready. As a team we were nervous because this was our only shot, and he was coming with us dead or alive.

My team and I were up and ready to go by 2 am in case he decided to get there earlier. At around 3:50 a.m., I got the call from our girl. My PSD team and I jumped in the truck and we were off. As we pulled up a few of his guys were standing outside of the house. We used heavy gunfire on them and they ran away. We stormed into the house. We had one minute to ninety seconds to grab him and throw him in our truck dead or alive. As we got into the house we found him in the living room with our girl. He didn't expect us one bit and he didn't resist. We zip tied his hands behind his back and the four of us carried him and threw him into the bed of our truck. The girl ran with us and jumped into our truck also. As we got about one mile away from the house, driving back to the base, we had gun fire on us. We drove as fast as we could, never stopping for one second. At last we got back to the base. The soldiers at the base had a room ready for him with a hook in the ceiling. We hung the bastard upside down by his feet. The PSD team beat the shit out of him for all the soldiers' lives he had taken.

My commander came in later that morning and I told him I had a surprise for him. I walked him in and showed him our trophy!

My commander asked us, "Who the hell is this?"

I told him, "That's the Fox."

My commander was shocked. He couldn't believe how a prostitute could bring down a terrorist. He shook his head in disbelief. This guy was not only wanted by us, but by the U.S. too. He was a real scum bag. By getting him, his organization became very dysfunctional.

Later in the day we put him on the back of our truck tied up with only his underwear on and beaten. We drove for the first time in a long time down the streets and through the market. This was our first run for re-establishing the patrolling. We wanted to show everyone we were in control. The business people in the area couldn't believe it. My soldiers got out of the truck and bought water from the market. Never before could this have happened. We told the business people they don't have to pay us a percentage. We asked them instead to work with us to keep the streets safe for everyone. After our victory here, my PSD team and I went back to the MOD. My commander returned as well and a new commander was assigned there to finish re-building the battalion.

As I returned back to the MOD my fan club of terrorists there was looking for me and asking about me. They thought I never left the base, but little did they know. They had no idea where I was from or who my family was. Officials from the Iraqi government would keep requesting to have me brought in for an investigation or an official meeting. I would always ask them why because I had never done anything wrong and there was nothing to be discussed. I did my job by the book. They stated it was because my soldiers at the check point kept disrespecting the officers and their people. They kept coming up with stuff to try to bring me in. I knew if they brought me in they would execute me on the spot. They kept putting a lot of pressure on me and the PSD team to bring me in. But my PSD team never caved into their pressure.

The Islamic State Wants Me Dead

The corrupt government started creating situations, stating I had done something and trying to accuse me of a particular situation. They would accuse my guys of things while searching their guys at the check point. They also tried to accuse me of hurting one of their guys who came to my check point and out right punched one of my soldiers in the face for searching him. I had to take the guy down for assaulting one of my soldiers. The soldier was only doing his job. It was an absolute set up and they were doing anything they could to get rid of me.

There were a lot of al-Qaeda and Islamic State members in the Iraqi Government at the time. They had a lot of power and would try to use all the power they could. During this time the corrupt Iraqi government and the al-

Qaeda members in the government assigned a person to come and get me. They wanted me brought back to an unknown Iraqi government location in the red zone. The person who was assigned to me was Col. Mezher. I had known Mezher prior to the military and remembered him very well. He was a major in the naval intelligence during Saddam's time and he hated the Americans with a passion. Col. Mezher lived down the road from where I grew up. He owned an office supply store in my neighborhood. I used to buy my books for school from him. He didn't recognize me though because it was years ago when I was a kid and that was a good thing for me. I refused to go with Col. Mezher and leave the MOD. There was a huge fight between my commander and Col. Mezher's authorities. Once I figured out Col. Mezher's intentions I told my commander to let me handle this. My commander was very worried for me because Col. Mezher was a corrupt person. He also said Col. Mezher was working with al Qaeda. I knew they were coming for me. This was no surprise, but since I knew him I had one more surprise up my sleeve for Col. Mezher.

I had learned when you work with wild animals you would have to hold them away from you at an arms or more distance so they couldn't attack you. This rang true when working with and handling the terrorists, too. Col. Mezher was a professional man with his uniform on. But once the uniform came off or he broke from his professional role he became a very nasty individual. From there my PSD team and I went out to make sure Col. Mezher and his family still lived in the area and the house I last knew. And sure enough they did.

My PSD team and I came up with a plan to do one last mission. I knew this would be my last one because after this I would have to run for my life and so would my team. All good things do come to an end I hate to say. My PSD team told me to run and get the hell out. I knew my time was up but I needed to find out a little more information before I left. The next morning came and I told my PSD team when they had Col Mezher's family to let me know. My PSD team arrived in front of his house. At the same time Col. Mezher was trying to get me to his office with an official order. I knew there was no investigation or meeting. This was a fake invitation to my official assassination. This time I was ready. I was not afraid to go to Col. Mezher's office in the MOD. So as I started walking into Col. Mezher's office, my PSD team entered into his home. Col. Mezher didn't know what I was capable of. As I got to Mezher's office I got the call telling me I was all set. This mean the PSD team had Mezher's wife, daughters and son. As I got to Col. Mezher's office I said to him, "I am here to surrender! Are you ready to take me to the investigation?"

He said, "Absolutely let's go!" As he got up from his seat, he grabbed my left arm by my uniform real nasty and started tugging on my uniform. His face changed. You could see this wild animal inside of him start to come out. He said to me, "I will crush your head with my shoes after I kill you," as he gritted his teeth.

I looked him in the eye with sheer disgust and I said "Okay, but before we go, I think you should call your wife Shama before you kill me." He froze when I said his wife's name. He looked at me like he couldn't believe what I said.

I said, "Understand I could have run away, but before we go I will tell you this. In just five minutes, your family will be slaughtered after you put a bullet in my head. My mother will cry for me after you do this, but you will lose your entire family!"

He looked at me with disbelief, and I looked back at him with extreme confidence. I asked him, "Would you like to give Shama a call? Go ahead call her!"

As he picked up the phone and called her, my PSD guy answered the phone. He answered, "What do you want asshole?" My PSD guy put her on the phone so she could speak to her husband. She told Mezher my guys had her and the kids tied up. She explained to him they were going to kill her and the kids. He gave me back the phone.

I said to my PSD guy, "If you don't hear from me in three minutes you know what to do." Mezher sat down. I said, "What's wrong? You guys aren't used to losing? See how it feels to have terrorism come into your own home. Right now I look at this like a chess game and I say, "Check mate! You may think you are winning, but I can tell you you're losing big. My mother will have other family members to console her, but you'll have nothing left."

I looked at Col. Mezher and he said to me, "We can forget about the investigation please don't kill my family."

I responded back to him, "Do you think I want to kill your family? What I want to know is who wants me dead?"

He looked at me like he didn't know what to say. I said, "You have no idea how I know you... You used to sell books to me as a kid... I could have killed you any time I wanted to." He still didn't say a word. All he did was look at me. So I asked him again, "Who wants me dead? I do believe we're running out of time. There's only three minutes left."

He replied, "al Tanzeem." This meant "the organization." He asked me, "Why do you work for the Americans? You don't have to work for them. We could have given you money and moved you to any country you wanted if you stopped working for them. You're Iraqi and they don't give a shit about you."

I answered, "Fuck You! I would never take money from you. Which organization is it? Seems to me you don't want to see your family today!"

He looked at me again, He was so reluctant to tell me. And then he said "The Islamic State."

I realize he was reluctant to tell me because they could take him out for telling me and not following their orders of killing me.

I said to him, "Being corrupt and killing is not something I am willing to do. The Americans symbolize freedom and I want freedom. You think you're free when someone is ordering you to kill me and you have to follow their every word?" I didn't even wait for his answer. I walked out of his office and back to mine.

It was all clear now. The Islamic State was the group of ex-Iraqi military officers from Saddam's Regime who rejoined al-Qaeda and worked in the new Iraqi military. It made sense to me all these corrupt officials were tied to the Islamic State of Iraq.

After the meeting I walked back to my office and I called the PSD guys to tell them to let the family go and come back to the unit. I told them I had to leave fast and to hurry back. I hated always having to be mean and ugly, but it was the only way I could deal with these guys. You had to show them how it felt to be terrorized by bringing terrorism into their home and family. They had to get a taste of what they did to others. It would catch them off guard but it brought them down to the human level. Once you got them there you had a window of opportunity to try and reason with them.

13

My Time is Up

I realized at the time I had to do something because that was my last chance. There was no doubt they wanted me dead and I had to get out. After the meeting with Mezher I told the people in the U.S. intelligence agency I had to leave. I was living in danger in the MOD and if I didn't go I would be dead sooner than later. I had cheated death as long as I could. I went back to my room, burned papers and important information, packed up my stuff and moved myself into the green zone. When I entered the green zone I only had my two guns and a duffle bag. My whole PSD team cleared out also. They got transferred to different units in the military outside of Baghdad. We all left the MOD. No one stayed behind. The terrorists would never know where my PSD team or I went, or what happened to us. I knew they would come back after me and for sure they wouldn't let me get away. I also didn't want to put any of my soldiers or PSD team in danger. My soldiers were upset to see me leave because I wasn't there for them anymore. They respected me and I made sure I always took care of them. They knew and understood why I had to leave and I keep in touch with many of them still today.

At this point I continued working with the U.S. military. My job was patrolling with U.S. troops who needed interpreters. The U.S. intelligence agency knew where I was and I kept supplying them with information. I contacted LTC Burke to tell him I needed my papers in order because I needed to leave the country. I told him there was no place for me in this country anymore. LTC Burke got LT. Jason Faler on my paper work and it was later signed off by Brigadier General Michael Sweezey. The Iraqi unit I was attached to was right next to the green zone. I would work for the U.S. and go out on missions with them and in addition I would work for the Iraqi army too once in a while. After the whole Mezher ordeal I was transferred to a different Iraqi Unit. My name was on paperwork there but the commanders in that Iraqi unit knew my situation and didn't expect me to show up. I would show up for an hour or two every few weeks. I slept and lived on the American base. I was working in two different places and the Iraqi army didn't know I was working with both sides. At this point I was trying to keep a very low profile to buy time until my paperwork came through. I was still worried every day the terrorists from the MOD would find me.

One day I was walking through the American Base on my way to the PX when I accidentally walked past two Iraqi Generals who were at the base being escorted by U.S. Military members. I never expected to see them in there because they have no business being in there. A military advisor had escorted them and brought them inside the base. They looked right at me. Believe me I was well known with all these generals for what I had done by foiling both plots of theirs to kill Americans. I prayed they didn't recognize me.

They Caught Up to Me

A few days later I was out patrolling with a mixed unit of both American and Iraqi units, in a pretty safe area. Our unit, unknown to us, was being tracked by the terrorists and before we knew it we were under attack. An IED is what got me. I got up after being hit and fell right back down. I remember being hit and the helicopter transferring me to the U.S. combat hospital in the green zone. The next thing I remember was waking up in the hospital. I was injured but alive. I did end up having to have surgery and I stayed in the hospital for a little while. I got in touch with the intelligence officers I was working for the day after the surgery to let them know I was there and what had happened.

The surgeon who helped me was Dr. William Ralston. He was an amazing surgeon and he did an amazing job taking care of me. I will always be grateful to him for his outstanding work.

The intelligence officers instructed the hospital staff not to release my identity under any circumstances and if anyone asked about me to tell them I had died. People would come to the front gate of the hospital all the time and ask about people who were there. The terrorists were successful in getting me and now it was only a matter of time before they would send someone to snoop around and find out if they were successful in killing me. I needed them to believe I was dead. I was told a few days later someone had been around asking about me. The hospital was a very safe place for me, but I could not be identified by anyone. I was still waiting to hear if my paper work was done. Unknown to me, LTC Burke kept trying to get in touch with me. I was not returning his calls or e-mails so he became very worried. I was able to get a nurse to check my e-mail account and see if I had any important e-mails. She had reported back to me LTC Burke had been trying to e-mail me and my papers were ready. I had gotten my ticket out and I could head to the U.S! I got in contact with LTC Burke as fast as I could. I explained to him what had happened and he knew they would get me sooner or later. But I had gotten my papers to go and I would be out of there soon. A few days later, when I was ready to leave the hospital I went back to the American Base. I hid at the base for a short period of time so no one would see me until my plane ticket was ready. When the time came for me to fly out, the intelligence officers got a black hawk to take me to the airport where I would board a plane and fly to Turkey. From Turkey, I would fly to the U.S. In September 2008 I arrived at JFK airport in New York City. I was out and I was never going back. I had beaten them.

Corruption is All Over

Iraq was my home. Imagine yourself having to leave your country, which is all you've ever known. In 2003 Iraq seemed full of promise for the first time ever for me. I felt like life could be good there. We would have freedom and we would be able to achieve our dreams and have a normal life. But as time went on from 2003 to 2008 the government of Iraq was a bunch of thieves who put suits on every day. All these corrupt people started to come back and take all the high positions in the government. How is it the Americans had run our country fine and upon handing it back to the Iraqi government nothing ran right? This proved the corruption time and time again. These bull shit government officials did not want order or a successful future. You could smell the corruption on them and see their corruptness a mile away. Once the Iraqis took over the leadership, all the logistics of the military fell apart. One day we heard an Iraqi division commander, Brigadier General Fuad, stole all the salaries of his division and left the country with it. There were numerous times when the Iraqi army had no ammunition, no food or supplies. Things were getting worse as time went on. For me, I had to go. I hated leaving my family behind. What would happen to them? How would they live here? I left all my friends and family to start a new life in a new country. Many of my friends were killed in combat. Members of my PSD team and my soldiers were abducted and most likely executed. Today I look at my PSD team picture from the time we graduated PSD School and I can count on one hand how many are still alive. My whole time in the military with my team, we were always fighting two battles. The two battles were between the enemy at the front line of the battle and corrupted leadership in the back. The Iraqi parliament members brought the worst people from both sides, Shiites and Sunnis. This shit was going to represent the country and fill these high level positions. The people of Iraq would have elections and vote for parliament members based of their ethnicity, family tribe and religious belief. They didn't look to see if the parliament members had their best interests in mind. Things were getting very hectic and the Americans were turning over the country faster than they should have. All anti-American groups and terrorist organizations were happy to see the Americans do this because they couldn't wait to get control back. This was the perfect opportunity because the Iraqi army was weak, not very well supplied and full of corruption. It got to the point most terrorists who were detained by the Iraqi army were getting released because money was paid to the Iraqi government or a leader in the Iraqi military. You could see the writing on the wall. Iraq was a time bomb waiting to go off. The Prime Minister Al Malaki thought he could control it, but he wasn't in control much. Not to mention the amount of corruption he played a part in. He participated in contract scams and hiding money. At this point the terrorists didn't have to hide, and they were occupying very effective positions within Al Malaki's own government. The Iraqi government had to be divided between the Shiites and the Sunnis, but this didn't mean it brought in the right people. The terrorists were starting to infiltrate the government back in the beginning of 2005. Before this, the government was decent. When America had troops on the ground and was running our government, it paralyzed the corruption due to the pressure being placed on them. The terrorist infrastructure became very weak with the Americans there. If a terrorist got arrested by the U.S. military, there was no way out for them. Now with the Iraqis having more governmental control after 2008, if they were arrested, they had an easy "get out of jail free" card. The Iraqi government always practiced these types of negotiations, even back during Saddam times, but once the Americans got them it wasn't so easy. To this day this same shit goes on every day. The military captures them and the government releases them when they see cash. When you have your soldiers fighting in a battle and there is a huge shortage of logistics and the enemy is getting stronger and stronger by the day it's a matter of time before the soldiers and the army fall apart.

14

The Rebirth of ISIS

I start this section with a quote from President George W. Bush back on July 12, 2007 when he was addressing the American people about Iraq:

"I know some in Washington would like us to start leaving Iraq now! Begin withdrawing before our commanders tell us we are ready, would be dangerous.... For Iraq, for the region and for the United States. It would mean surrendering the future of Iraq to al-Qaeda. It would mean we would be risking mass killings on a horrific scale. It means we would allow the terrorists to establish a safe haven in Iraq to replace the one they lost in Afghanistan. It would mean increasing the probability that American troops would have to return at some later date to confront an enemy that is even more dangerous."

It was like President Bush had a crystal ball and could see the future. I understand very well many people didn't like Bush, but this is not about Democrats or Republicans and who is right or wrong. The threat ISIS presents today is a threat against humanity. It is a battle against all of humanity. It's not a battle about faith. It's a battle for power. They are not looking to be in Iraq, but to be on every continent in the world. Today ISIS is starting to pop up all over the world and in different cities. They pose a threat to humanity all over the world. Innocent people are dying so they can show how powerful and dangerous they are. They want to run the world! That is their goal and this is what they are brainwashing people with and promising them in order to recruit them.

Back in 2004, al-Qaeda was led by al Zirkaui in Iraq. Bin Laden was the main leader of al-Qaeda overall. After the death of al Zirkaui in 2006, al-Qaeda in Iraq was made up of and led by native people. Al Zirkaui was Jordanian and during the time he led al-Qaeda he was surrounded by many native Iraqis. At this time al-Qaeda in Iraq was calling themselves the Islamic state of Iraq. The Islamic State of Iraq was not only made up of native Iraqis, but it was also made up of many ex-Iraqi military members which joined them from other terrorist groups. That is why the organization, according to Col. Mezher, was the Islamic State who wanted me dead. Which meant al-Qaeda. The Islamic State was a much more intelligent group of people than the rest of al-

Qaeda in my opinion. They were much more educated military-wise because most of them had served in Saddam's regime. They were not as well-known as the rest of the al-Qaeda groups were. There is a difference between terrorists who blow themselves up and a terrorist who leads, plans and executes. By killing the terrorists who blow themselves up or killing the terrorists in the street fighting you, you are not going to be able to stop them because they can always bring more fighters. Also, they are not the head people coming up with and executing the plans. When you kill a leader it creates chaos in the organization and they become more vulnerable.

In June 2006 al-Qaeda was being run by Abu Ayyub al-Masri. This was after al Zarqawi's death. He held the position of being the leader of al-Qaeda until April 2010. And another person named Abu Omar al-Baghdadi was named the leader of al-Qaeda. But he was never a real person. The Iraqi Minister of the Interior thought he was killed, but in reality al-Qaeda had put a fictitious face as the leader of their organization. I believe al-Qaeda did this because they were going through a very bad time. A large majority of their most dangerous fighters were jailed. This put al-Qaeda at a weak point. In June 2014 a new leader had been announced. He was now the leader of ISIS and no longer the leader of al-Qaeda. Abu Bakr al Baghdadi was and is still the present leader of ISIS.

Back in the day, Abu Bakr al Baghdadi was a mosque clerk in Iraq. He was jailed in the American prisons back in 2004 and he was released as a low level prisoner. He was elected to be the leader by the people he was in jail with. One of his big goals during his reign was to free all the members of al-Qaeda and the members of the Islamic State. That is why the al-Qaeda members announced this fake guy as the new leader to throw everyone off. They started to establish communication lines with the prisoners inside the prisons. Al Baghdadi didn't want what was going on inside the jails to be made public, because they were making one of their greatest plans of all time. Al Baghdadi and the prisoners he was in communication with re-organized and planned what they would do. He promised the prisoners he would get them out of jail. During the first term for President Obama, he announced he was going to be bringing the American soldiers home by the end of 2011. The new leader didn't believe this. But, if it was true it would make their life and their plans of what they wanted to do a lot easier. Prisons all over Iraq were being attacked from the end of 2011 thru 2013. This was after the Americans pulled out and took their hands away. While the Americans were in charge of the prisons, no prisoners escaped. All this hard work the Americans had done was lost when it was handed over to the Iraqis. The prisons were being attacked because Abu Bakr needed to rebuild the infrastructure of the Islamic State and he needed those prisoners to accomplish it. The prisoners who were jailed inside the prisons were very dangerous people and very strong operatives. In June 2011, forty-seven prisoners escaped from a prison in Mosul. April 27, 2012, one hundred and two detainees escaped from a prison in Tikrit. Of those one hundred and two prisoners, forty-seven of them were al Qaeda operatives. One terrorist who escaped at this time, Shaker Wahib al-Fahdawi (Abu Waheeb), was a well-known terrorist the Americans had arrested in 2006. He was transferred to Tikrit, to the prison there to be sentenced to death. He was freed on April 27, 2012 and now he is one of the main leaders and dangerous field commanders of ISIS. In 2012, at a prison in Baghdad, a prisoner was able to build a suicide belt and free more prisoners. This was a perfect demonstration of the corruption going on. How would a prisoner get the supplies to build this? The supplies and weapons would be brought in hidden under food. Families of the detainees would place weapons in an area under food inside the food container. Iraqis were not smart enough to check the food, or they were given some money to look the other way. One of the biggest attacks on a prison was in July 2013 on the Abu Ghraib prison located outside of Baghdad. It is an unknown number of prisoners who escaped. Iraqi intelligence states it was six hundred. But it is listed to be between five hundred to one thousand prisoners that escaped. Now hundreds of these guys were free, Abu Bakr had the people he needed to rebuild the infrastructure. With all these escaped terrorists and operatives you now have your star-studded line up of what ISIS is today. Abu Bakr was successful in rebuilding the infrastructure and ISIS was complete. Back in 2007 Iraq was quiet and the level of violence had calmed down. The reason why was because all these terrorists were in jail. America had worked hard to capture all these guys and now they were out and free.

There were times between 2012 and 2013 I would speak to my PSD team members and soldiers who were still in the military. They would tell me how much bigger the training camps had gotten and how much stronger and more organized this terrorist organization was. A large terrorist training camp had been found in the middle of a desert. It was an unexpected find by the Iraqi military on a routine helicopter patrol. They were nervous about this. They didn't know what kind of a battle to expect in the future. But nothing had changed. The corruption was the same in the military and they would have to deal with it as it came.

The Weak Iraqi Army

The Iraqi government and the army didn't have the ability to stand up to ISIS because the corrupt Iraqi officials had put them in such a weak state. Like I said before, back in 2012 and 2013 my old soldiers and PSD team would tell me how much more organized ISIS was and how many more members they had. It was the corrupt officials and the money they supported them with that made ISIS so much stronger. My guys were nervous about ISIS and they didn't know how they would fight them. Based upon what my soldiers tell me who are still in combat today, ISIS had no problem winning the battle against them. The reason for this is because my military guys would capture them, put them in prison and they would be released a few days later by the corrupt Iraqi officials. If one of my military guys got captured they would be executed right where they stood. The Iraqi army had a very difficult time delivering battle logistics and tactics they were going to use because this information would be leaked. So ISIS would show up before the Iraqi army did and they would ambush them. The Iraqi army was getting slaughtered and the morale in the army went to zero. Soldiers would be surrounded by ISIS for days with no food, water or ammunition. So these battles would end up not about fighting for liberating land but instead fighting for their survival. The soldiers suffered from the betrayal in the Iraqi leadership. One of the biggest mass killings of Iraqi soldiers happened within the last half of 2014. Seventeen hundred Iraqi soldiers were shot in the head to death by ISIS, in Tikrit, Iraq. The soldiers were ordered to leave their base in civilian clothes by Iraqi Colonel Ayub. He told them they had to leave the base because they were no longer serving at this base and they were being moved to Baghdad. Prior to this he kept encouraging them to leave the base unarmed. None the less, the soldiers were happy to be going back to Baghdad to be closer to home. As these young men left the base they had no idea ISIS was waiting for them down the road. ISIS captured them and shot almost all of them. There were only a few survivors. Those survivors either ran away, or the shot to their head didn't kill them. Around half of these young men ISIS lined up next to a river. If they tried to run away ISIS would kill them. Each man was taken one by one, turned to face the river and shot in the back of the head and their body was thrown into the river. The other half of the men were taken to the dessert, lined up next to trenches and shot in the head. A few of these young men who survived have been interviewed and gave information about ISIS. This caused the Iraqi Army to collapse from the inside. The soldiers could not trust their leaders. They were fighting the enemy with no resources and the future of the military was being wiped away. The battles were always a win-win for ISIS. The Iraqi leaders who were in charge of these seventeen hundred young men were now put under investigation. They claimed they never ordered these soldiers to leave the base. The Iraqi government blamed it on anyone they could because they had to answer to the families whose sons they had lost. This was the largest massacre of soldiers in modern day Iraq.

An Army of Investments

There are so many questions being asked about all the money that has been stolen and where it went to by the soldiers in the Iraqi army. The Iraqi soldiers who are doing their job everyday have not been paid in over seventy five days as of March 2015.

Where did this corruption come from for this disaster to happen? The answer is that corruption and stealing was a common practice by the Iraqi Military officials and generals under Saddam. These ugly gentleman had run away when the Americans came but were now again holding positions in the new Iraqi military but using the old practices. A person who is a great example of this is General Mohan. Guys like Mohan were both the past and present Iraqi Army leaders. For the corrupt Iraqi officials it was not about leading the army or promoting who was more qualified. Instead it was a fight between political parties over who would be the leader for a specific division and how much money they could take. Different political parties and militias who were outsiders and not part of the Iraqi army would also want to be in the decision process for who was to become division commander. These different groups had no business making any decisions like this. Monetary bribes in the amount of five hundred thousand dollars or more would be given to the big Iraqi leader in the MOD to obtain a specific position like a brigade commander or division commander. Their motivation for doing this was so they could steal the salaries of soldiers. The five hundred thousand dollars they paid would end up becoming such a very lucrative investment it would put most Wall Street investors to shame.

There is a video on You Tube of an Iraqi Major General who is being interviewed after he left the Iraqi Army. He was a commander of troops in Mosul. He happened to be a good commander and not a corrupt one. In the video he explains how he only had about six thousand soldiers and police on the ground working which he knew of. His roster on the other hand said he had over thirty thousand troops. When I was in the Iraqi army we each got paid equal to eight hundred dollars per month. So if you multiply eight hundred dollars with thirty thousand soldiers and you would come to twenty-four million dollars per month. Now if you got paid for soldiers who died, or had soldiers stay home and you only had to pay them half their salary, this would be a fantastic investment. And yes soldiers were paid half of their salary to stay home so the terrorists could take over. As a division commander you would charge twenty-four million dollars per month and only maybe have to pay five million out of it. So you came out with a profit of nineteen million per month. Not a bad return on your five hundred thousand dollar investment. The amount of money that would be stolen each month is unimaginable. How could this be? This is the truth.

There is this type of corruption going on today. The commander being interviewed left Mosul and the military all together. Over half of the soldiers he had under him were loyal to ISIS. How can anyone fight ISIS when there is such loyalty and so much money being handed around?

In the beginning, the corruption and money was a secret no one knew about. Now everyone knows. So the parliament members would suggest who they wanted for the division commanders. They suggested these people because they were loyal to some political party. I left Iraq in 2008. I found out a couple of years ago I was still getting paid as a soldier in the Iraqi army. Who was getting my salary? I couldn't tell you but it wasn't me for sure! One thing I can tell you is there is no way of stopping it. With the current situation in Iraq as of March 2015 the only answer the soldiers are being given is that they do not know where the money has gone and that they have opened an investigation. Of course they know where the money has gone. So now these poor guys have to go to work and not get paid. Their options at this time are to keep fighting ISIS to protect their families, towns and cities, or to put their guns down and let ISIS invade. They have chosen to keep fighting even though they are suffering because they want ISIS out.

ISIS Victories

In Mosul, ISIS was successful in gaining control of the whole state within minutes. One would say how could this be? I am sad to report it is the truth. In Mosul there was a whole Iraqi Army division and an Iraqi National Police Unit. And, between those who two groups, there was supposed to be at least thirty thousand members in the Iraqi forces and those numbers were not even close to being accurate. Remember I told you about the Commander who stated he only had about six thousand troops and many were loyal to ISIS. With those facts one can see how it didn't take much to take over Mosul. The Iraqi corrupt military leaders at the time ordered the Iraqi troops to pull out of Mosul allowing ISIS to walk right in. The Iraqi government did not understand why the troops were pulled out. There was no order from the government to do such a thing. The government also found out there were only six thousand Iraqi force members all together. The government finally saw the truth that they were paying salaries for thirty thousand members like the Major General stated. With this truth now exposed, the Iraqi government asked themselves where had all the money gone? Who was taking it? This is how deep the corruption is in the Iraqi government. Here Al Malaki was the prime minister and he was paying and fighting ISIS with troops he didn't even have. Al Malaki was someone who liked having power. He blamed the failure of the Iraqi army on not being able to choose his own cabinet and the people he appointed were forced on him. Of course bad people are going to force in more bad people. They had an agenda. The corruption and betrayal in the Iraqi government was at an all-time high with ISIS supporters. This new Iraqi Army had the most unlucky soldiers on the earth. This is why they would be surrounded for five to six days at a time by ISIS. There was no help or support for them. The Americans left way too soon and the transition was pre-mature and done too fast. Iraq collapsed due to the early pull out of the United States. Handing over the authority of the country to the Iraqis was done too soon and too premature. The anti-American groups felt this transition was perfect for them. They knew the Iraqi government was too fragile and nowhere near mature or established enough yet. ISIS at present still has control over Mosul and a few other provinces around Mosul. ISIS believes beheading young men who don't agree with them is okay. They also feel taking eight year old girls as their wives is okay too. ISIS is not only doing a fantastic job of recruiting foreign fighters, but they have taken young boys ages eight to thirteen, and started training them too. They are brain washing people from all over the world and the young Iraqi boys. A new generation of ISIS is in the making and soon there will be another Afghanistan. All kinds of nationalities and ethnicities are being recruited Chinese, Tunisians, Germans, Moroccans, Europeans, Americans, Australians, Saudi Arabians and many more. How do I know this? I know because my old PSD team and troops are fighting on the front lines today against ISIS. I speak to them every day. They tell me what is going on and not the media. I hear and see the truth. I can call or message any one of them at any moment. My old team knows this for a fact because they pull the passports and IDs off the dead ISIS fighters. They know where the fighters are coming from. In recent weeks ISIS has started pulling the passports and IDs of these fighters before they go out to fight. ISIS now doesn't want people knowing where they are coming from. The Sunni extremists are telling these foreigners the Islamic State will rule the world and ISIS has started relying more on these foreign fighters. Now the Islamic State expanded way too fast and now these Islamic state fighters are even threatening their own countries.

Crowds of People

A supreme religious leader of the Shiite people in Iraq had given an order for all the southern states to arm themselves and send their men to fight side by side with the Iraqi military. Thousands of Iraqi citizens from the south of Iraq went to fight with the Iraqi Military. They call themselves the "Crowds of People" and they are Shiites. Some of the members of the Crowds of People are old militia members from Shiite militias who fought the American and Iraqi armies before. So this proves Iraq has been put in an awkward position because it is looking for all kinds of help. But, it also proves everyone wants to fight ISIS and agrees ISIS is against humanity and should not be allowed to exist. Even the enemies of the Iraqi army are working with them today to get rid of ISIS. The one stipulation the Crowds of People has is that they have their own rules and do not follow the military's rules. These fighters, once they get a hold of an ISIS fighter, execute him on the spot. There are no prisoners. The Iraqi soldiers now also are executing the ISIS members on their own. If they don't, the corrupt authorities will allow the ISIS members to be released. And since the soldiers are no longer getting paid by the government they don't need to follow the rules.

Back in the day when I was in charge and in the field, when I captured a terrorist, an Iraqi Parliament member would call me and tell me to let them go. Because the terrorist belonged to him. This was all due to the corruption. They would threaten me if I didn't let them go, and it would affect my leadership because my leadership position was supposed to obey the higher authority. So I would tell my troops to execute the terrorist when they captured him so there was no live individual brought back to the base. If the terrorist was brought before a judge, the judge would let him go because the judge would either be threatened, his daughter would be killed, or they would offer him money.

15

How to Defeat ISIS

The biggest thing most people do not realize is ISIS is divided into two different groups, foreigners and natives. The foreigners are the ones who have been recruited from all over the world. They are all nationalities and they can speak many different languages. Their one big disadvantage for the foreign fighters is they are not familiar with the land they are fighting on. This makes them an easy target. The native guys know their land and cities very well. They are the ones who lead the foreigners in the fight. They host the foreign fighters and show them around. In today's battle everybody is so worried about bombing wherever ISIS is. You can bomb as many foreign fighters as you want, but the next day ISIS will have their strong force of foreign fighters back. There is a line of foreign fighters waiting to come and fight. Finding replacements for ISIS is not hard. Therefore, the natives are the ones who have to be taken out. If a jihadi extremist from Belgium shows up, he doesn't know his way around. So who takes him around? A native fighter! Without these native fighters, the foreigners would not know their way around or know which direction to take the battle. They would never know how to launch an attack or in what direction they should attack. The native fighters are the heart of ISIS in these primary ISIS areas. ISIS does not go to a place where they do not have allies. ISIS shows up where there are native supporters.

There has been a lot of misinformation on ISIS. What ISIS wants is to make the battle sound like it is Sunnis versus Shiites. But it's not true. The media has also taken this message and made it look like it's a religious battle. This is not reality either. The media is trying to make it look like ISIS is representing all Sunnis but this is not a correct representation. If you look at the battle against ISIS you have Sunnis, Shiites and Christians all working together to fight against them. They are all dying together fighting against ISIS. This has been the greatest unity ever in Iraq in many years. There have been plenty of Sunni's who have stood up to ISIS and not allowed them to come into their villages. There are Sheiks in the Fallujah and Ramadi area who refuse to let them come in and have lost close to four hundred of their men fighting against ISIS. These men have never been shown on the media or gotten any credit or respect for what they have done. ISIS is trying to show everyone they are fighting a religious war. By the average person listening to this and thinking this way, ISIS and al-Qaeda have achieved the reputation they want to represent. They want to you to think every Muslim is like them. They want everyone to think less of Muslims so hate will be generated between Muslims and the general population. Then once the public opinion changes these Muslims will become allies of ISIS. The truth of what's happening in Iraq right now is it's a fight against the extremists. The extremists believe no one should live if they do not have the same beliefs as them. They want to kill all Sunnis who don't follow them, and the same goes for all Shiites and all Christians. But ISIS and this extreme thinking is not the majority in Iraq. There is never a positive side of a situation shown. It is always the negative side. They never show how the people have defeated ISIS and pushed ISIS out of their towns, or show how they have stood up and refused ISIS. The media is only showing what ISIS and al-Qaeda want shown to keep everyone in fear. Fear is the greatest controller. The scariest weapon ISIS uses today is media. When it comes to the field battle ISIS is not as big as they look on TV. The soldiers fighting them today on the ground have had battles with them, but there were not as many ISIS members to fight because there were not as many members as there appeared to be. ISIS uses the media to frighten the American public and the world. This way they will get everyone to hate Muslims and make you think your Muslim neighbor has the same beliefs as the ISIS members. I have been asked what is the difference between the extremist Muslim and an average Muslim? The difference is an extremist Muslim is a person who doesn't accept diversity and refuses to acknowledge your existence. There are not many Muslims who follows those beliefs. The average Muslim accepts diversity and allows their children go to the same schools as your children do. They also walk around the same malls as you do and eat at some of the same restaurants you so. They are very accepting of diversity and your beliefs and laws. They are not extremists. But the world and its people hate Muslims because they are shown that all Muslims represent ISIS and hate everyone else in the world. The goals which ISIS and the extremists set out to achieve have been accomplished. If they can get those average Muslims to hate the world and its people because of how they are being treated, than ISIS and the extremists now have new allies, and they can now enter into towns and cities they weren't able to get into before. Hence they have now started to take over the world, which is what they want.

There should be a law in Iraq like there is in America where there is a strict policy on no negotiating with terrorists. You cannot negotiate with people who do not have the same beliefs as you do when all they want to do is kill you. There is evil everywhere. I have always said that the evil people in Iraq end up being celebrities over here. And, that's because they are the same ten people shown over and over again on TV and in the media. Imagine you are shown thugs from America over and over again, in an unsafe neighborhood. Over time, the people watching this are going to start to believe America is all crime and not a good place to live.

When the Syrian civil war started in Syria. ISIS started to fight side by side with the Sunni rebels there because they were allies. The same goes today in Iraq. ISIS showed up in Mosul because there were a lot of allies living there. These native Islamic extremists become the new authority in their city and they make their own rules for everyone to follow. Today in Mosul a large majority of the Iraqi tribes committed their loyalty to ISIS. ISIS has also been showing up in different countries all over the world because they have allies there.

To defeat ISIS today one of the first things to be done is to hit the engine and the heart of ISIS movements. The engine and the heart of ISIS is the native fighters. This war is not a heavy weapon war only. This war is an intelligence war. If you look at the Iraqi capabilities intelligence wise, they have zero intelligence. I don't even believe the Iraqis even have a drone to show them what the enemy has been doing ahead of them. So the Iraqis are not capable at all intelligence wise. These soldiers have the biggest heart and drive to fight them, but without intelligence it makes the fight tougher. I know for a fact their field intelligence is nothing but social media news. If you were to ask me how to get ISIS out of Mosul today, which was a question I was asked by my soldiers in the field, I would say to go take out the native fighters.

The big question now is how do we take the natives down? The one thing I advised my soldiers to do was to use social media. About ninety-nine percent of those native fighters are either on Facebook or Twitter posting daily updates and pictures of the Islamic State's occupied areas. Some ISIS members even use Facebook as a mode of communication. They use it to message and chat with each other, as well as show their location. If you use social media you're not looking at ghosts anymore, you have pictures and names. More often than not you can get locations of where they are. Now a list starts to form of all the natives. There are a lot of people within the ISIS occupied area who are willing to help the military. And no one has taken advantage of this. This needs to be done before one soldier is moved into any occupied area. Once the native ISIS fighters are not secure anymore you will see ISIS weaken. A technique I advised my soldiers to use was to post the pictures of all the native fighters on social media and to make them "Wanted." Let them know they will be executed as soon as the military gets there. Not every terrorist is willing to die. There are many of them who love their lives more than anything. One other thing. What about their families when their pictures are all over the place and they are being wanted? Not only will those individuals not be secure but their families will not be secure either. When you expose their wives, children, parents and family in general it makes their family vulnerable to threats. Now you have taken some of the most dangerous ISIS fighters out of their comfort zone. I have heard when some of these steps were initiated by the Iraqi Military some of these terrorists had skipped town. They became afraid for their lives and their families' lives. Using social media is a great resource for the intelligence side of the battle.

Everything needed to fight a war takes a lot of money. Weapons, soldiers, military vehicles, ammunition, drones, explosives and technology all require extensive funding. Looking at today's situation in Iraq, the Iraqi soldiers lack those necessities to wage a strong fight. Especially an army who hasn't gotten paid in seventy five days. In my opinion, the volunteer fighters have better capabilities and resources over the Iraqi army itself. The militias who are fighting among the volunteers and Iraqi army may have better results than any other branches because of the support they have. But, before you hit ISIS with anything you need to break down their confidence. When ISIS broadcasts their beheadings and setting people on fire they are demonstrating how strong they are to us and the rest of the world. They are trying to make a statement that they cannot be beaten to scare people. You have to do the same back to them. The Iraqi soldiers have now started posting videos and pictures on social media of ISIS members getting executed or bodies lying dead after they were killed by the Iraqi military. By doing this they are showing ISIS can be defeated and they are breaking down the confidence of the ISIS fighters. Posting videos of executing native fighters and revealing their identity scares the native fighters. If you took a lot of these natives out of the fight because of fear, think about how much damage this would cause ISIS. It's like you are taking the eyes of these foreign fighters and you are making them blind. I remember when we used this kind of game back in Fallujah. At the time we didn't have social media and our tactics were a little different, but it forced the terrorists to run back to the country they came from.

A large social media campaign and attack is the least expensive and easiest tactic to fight ISIS. It is a great way to weaken the infrastructure of ISIS in a particular territory. When a point of weakness is identified you would bring in Special Forces. It has to be almost fought like Fallujah was fought. The Iraqis do have Special Forces who were trained by the Americans, but they were weakened and over-used by all the pressure placed on them. New fresh people have to be brought in. The whole city at this point would have to be evacuated so air strikes could take place, and teams of men would have to go door to door to flush out the fighters and allies left behind. This time we cannot let these foreign fighters run. These guys hate America and they hate freedom. They are enemy number one to America today. Iraq does have the amount of guys needed for the fight between the military, militias and The Crowds of People. What they lack is equipment, support and tactics. ISIS can be thrown out, but we cannot allow them to run away this time. They either have to be held very tight in prisons or be executed immediately like the Iraqis are doing now.

One of the most disgusting things ISIS has initiated now is called the "Sex Jihad." They have invited women from all over the earth to come and pleasure the ISIS fighters. My soldiers have caught people crossing the borders from Saudi Arabia into Iraq looking to join ISIS for sex. This was the most unbelievable thing I had ever heard. We didn't have this before. The big problem that this sex jihad has led to is fighters are coming for sex. This has led to the raping of women and children. Women have also been taken captive and sold as sex slaves and eight-year-old girls are being taken as wives. So as I have stated before, use their weaknesses against them. Every terrorist has a weakness. Set up traps. Rats love cheese and ISIS loves sex. This is their biggest weakness. Strategic operations can be set up where you can trap these disgusting bastards with women. There are many ways to infiltrate them. The plan has to be creative and very well thought out.

I have seen so much death, deceit and destruction. So many cities, villages and lands destroyed. I have seen evil at its worst. Evil does exist and it is very ugly. I have seen many good people die and many families be torn apart. And, at the end of it all, I sometimes ask myself what was it all for? What was gained? The next day comes and goes. Months and years go by. Numerous sacrifices made and memories many choose not to remember. Family has always been a very important thing to me. Protecting my family was always number one as it is for everyone else. As long as evil exists war will happen. The world powers will always agree to disagree. Everyone has a place on this earth. We were all put here for a reason. We have to find a way to co-exist and manage. I close my eyes at night feeling thankful many families out there have their loved ones still with them. I did my best to fight evil and save as many as I could. I wish there could have been more. I lost friends and family too. These days will forever be in my heart and have helped me become who I am today. I am grateful for all the men and women in the armed forces I was able to help and I am thankful I had the capabilities to do it. Every day when I walk down the street and see people in uniform I am reminded of the sacrifices they have made, and of mine.

Thank you

Made in the USA
Columbia, SC
07 June 2019